# Setting Goals That Count

## A Christian Perspective

# Also by Joe Allison

***Swords & Whetstones:***
   *A Guide to Christian Bible Study Resources*

***Spades & Pruning Hooks:***
   *A Guide to Christian Devotional Resources*

# Setting Goals That Count

## A Christian Perspective

### JOE ALLISON
*Author, Swords & Whetstones*

JORDAN*publishing*
*innovative christian resources*

Copyright © Joseph D. Allison. All rights reserved. Without limiting the rights under copyright here reserved, no part of this publication may be reproduced, stored in or introduced into a retrieval system, or transmitted, in any form or by any means (electronic, mechanical, photocopying, recording, or otherwise) without the prior written permission of the publisher. Please direct such requests to:

>  Rights and Permissions
>  Jordan Publishing
>  P.O. Box 3043
>  Anderson, Indiana 46018-3043
>
>  info@jordanpublishing.net

Unless otherwise noted, Scripture quotations are taken from the Holy Bible, NEW INTERNATIONAL VERSION®, NIV® Copyright © 1973, 1978, 1984, 2011 by Biblica, Inc.® Used by permission. All rights reserved worldwide.

Scripture quotations marked THE MESSAGE are taken from THE MESSAGE Copyright © by Eugene H. Peterson 1993, 1994, 1995, 1996, 2000, 2001, 2002. Used by permission of NavPress. All rights reserved. Represented by Tyndale House Publishers, Inc.

Scripture quotations marked TEV are taken from the Good News Translation (Today's English Version, Second Edition) © 1992 American Bible Society. All rights reserved.

Cover photo copyright © auremar / 123RF Stock Photo.

ISBN 978-1-891314-15-5 (Paperback)
ISBN 978-1-891314-09-4 (ePub)


Jordan Publishing titles are available through Amazon.com, BarnesandNoble.com, and other leading book retailers.

Printed in the United States of America by IngramSpark.

# Contents

Preface to Revised Edition ............................................. 6
1. Are You Setting Goals or Just Making Plans? ........... 7
2. How to Test Your Goals ............................................ 20
3. You *Can* Get There from Here .................................. 27
4. Building a Life Will Cost You Plenty! ...................... 34
5. Are You on Schedule? ............................................... 42
6. A Portrait of Your Dream ......................................... 51
7. Becoming What You Choose .................................... 65
8. Develop Your Abilities .............................................. 81
9. Discover Your Gifts ................................................... 90
10. When You Need to Change Your Plans ................ 100
11. Face Forward — It's Time to Start! ......................... 109

# Preface to Revised Edition

I was delighted to see the enthusiastic response to *Setting Goals That Count* when it was published by Chosen Books in 1985 and reissued in hardcover by Word Book Club. Three decades have passed, but there's a steady demand for used copies, even though some are priced at fifty dollars or more.

The time is right for a revised edition of the book, since many people are dealing with the same vocational dilemmas that emerged in the recession of the early 1980s. However, we have kept changes to a minimum because the book's core biblical teachings have not changed.

Most scripture quotations are now from the New International Version instead of the King James, several anecdotes have been updated, and we have cited a few quotations from more recent studies of human psychology. Otherwise the book is essentially as it first appeared.

May it continue to bless readers' lives, and may it challenge you to become all that God calls you to be.

Joe Allison<br>April, 2016

*We are always getting ready to live, but never living.*
— Ralph Waldo Emerson

# 1. Are You Setting Goals Or Just Making Plans?

A troubled man from my congregation poured out his frustrations. He had made a career of government service—over twenty years so far—and he had peaked early. Promotions eluded him. Regulations hamstrung him. Yet he said, "If I can hang on just a few more years I'll be able to retire. I don't want to lose my benefits."

He felt his job was a dead end. Many days, he just wanted to park his truck and walk away from everything. "I feel trapped," he said, "and I don't know how to get out."

"How old are you?"

"Fifty-three."

"Not that old. And you're in good health. Barring any accidents or unexpected illnesses, you should live past the average life expectancy for a man. That's about age seventy-eight. How old were your grandfathers when they died?"

"They were both in their mid-eighties."

"Then statistics say you'll probably live to your eighties, too. That means you may have nearly thirty years of healthy, productive life ahead of you. So what are you doing the rest of your life?"

His predicament is all too common. In our rush to make a livelihood, we Christians tend to forget our goals for life. So when we come to a critical juncture such as the last decade before retirement, we feel anxiety and fear. We don't know where we're going. We have no long-range goals.

This is why I believe we should study what God's Word says about our life goals. How does God say we should set long-range goals? How does he say we should reevaluate our goals when life changes drastically and unexpectedly? These are the questions we will tackle in this book.

You will find some practical tools for goal-setting as well as step-by-step procedures for reevaluating your life goals at crucial decision points, such as my friend was facing. More important, you will be challenged to consider how your daily plans fit into the big picture of lifelong goals. You will gain a fresh perspective on the way God reveals his will to you. In short, this is more than a nuts-and-bolts manual of life planning; it's an invitation to reassess your relationship with God.

A Christian does goal-setting and plan-making within the context of this relationship, while a non-Christian sets goals and makes crucial decisions without the benefit of it. We will come back to this matter repeatedly and test your aspirations against Scripture to see whether they are godly aspirations, because I'm convinced that we feel most satisfied when we strive to become the persons God created us to be.

### *Goals vs. Plans*

We ought to understand the difference between a goal and a plan, because it's easy to get the two confused. On New Year's Day, people often make resolutions for the year ahead. These are seldom goals; rather, they are plans. That is to say, they are methods for reaching a goal. I might tell you, for example, "I have a goal of losing weight this year."

"Exactly what do you have in mind?" you might ask.

"Well, I'm going to eat no more than a thousand calories a day." (That's not a goal; it's a plan. It's how I'm going to act in order to reach my goal.)

"How much weight do you hope to lose?"

"About thirty pounds." (Again, that's not a goal; it's a target that indicates I am making progress toward weight loss, just as losing ten pounds or twenty pounds would be targets.)

So you press me. "Why do you want to lose weight?"

"So that I'll be healthier," I say. "So that my body will be stronger. Perhaps I'll even live a bit longer by taking off some excess weight."

Now that is my goal! It is the end toward which I am aiming. It is the destination I am trying to reach. All the other steps—the menus, the exercise routines, the targets for each week's weight loss—are simply means for reaching my ultimate destination. That destination is my real goal.

For this reason, I'm not too upset if I forget my New Year's resolutions by Ground Hog's Day. I won't wring my hands and say, "I've failed again!" Because resolutions are not really my goals; they are simply plans for reaching my goals. And if one plan fails, I can try another.

Here is a good way to tell the difference between a plan and a goal: *Generally, we describe plans with "do" sentences and goals with "be" sentences.* Here are some sample New Year's resolutions; see if you can tell whether they are goals or plans:

- "I'm going to iron shirts every Monday morning."
- "I'm going to visit Aunt Sarah at the nursing home every week."
- "I'm going to take a course in accounting."

All of these are "do" sentences. Each one describes a method or strategy for reaching a goal. Now look at these revised resolutions:

- "I'm going to iron shirts every Monday morning so that I'll be a more efficient homemaker."
- "I'm going to visit Aunt Sarah every week so that I'll be a more faithful nephew."
- "I'm going to take a course in accounting so that I'll be a better bookkeeper."

See the difference? The "do" sentences describe a plan of action, while the "be" sentences describe the result of that action. A plan describes how you intend to reach your destination; but your goal *is* your destination.

Keep sight of your goals—what you intend to "be." Instead of thinking about what you will do in the next year, think about *who you will become*. That really is your goal.

I believe many of us are so busy with short-range plans that we don't take stock of our goals, or we are so absorbed with the daily strategies of living that we forget about our goals. As a result, we don't know if we have reached today's goals or if we are any closer to tomorrow's. We are obsessed with what we are going to *do*, so we don't consider who we are *becoming*. If you want to become the person God created you to be, you need to set goals before you start making plans.

### Heart vs. Mind

God influences a Christian's goal-setting and plan-making through what we might call a spiritual internal guidance system. When engineers launched the Voyager I spacecraft in 1977 to explore the solar system and beyond, they gave it a computerized internal guidance system because they knew they could not manually steer the probe as it flew farther and farther from earth. It's now more than twelve billion miles away, so our radio commands take more than sixteen hours to reach it. Although NASA's mission controllers occasionally send instructions to Voyager 1, they leave daily operations to its own internal guidance system.

God has given every one of us an internal guidance system, too. It's not electronic. It doesn't use computer chips or cables. But something within us is capable of receiving God's guidance, just as the Voyager I spacecraft receives course corrections from its command headquarters. The Bible calls this internal guidance system the "heart."

Granted, our hearts sometimes go wrong. We must take readings against God's Word and the counsel of other Christians to make sure we stay on God's true course. But God does steer us inwardly, so we should pay attention to our innermost aspirations. When our "hearts" are properly tuned to the Lord, they will point us toward serving him.

While Scripture uses the term *heart* to refer to our goal-setting, it uses the term *mind* to refer to our daily plan-making. One New Testament passage points out the difference between a person's heart and mind:

> This is the covenant I will establish with the people of Israel after that time, declares the Lord. I will put my laws in their minds and write them on their hearts. I will be their God, and they will be my people (Heb 8:10).

This verse suggests two distinct functions when it says God will "put" his law into his people's minds and "write" it upon their hearts. The word *put* suggests temporary change, while *write* indicates more permanent change. We observe this distinction in everyday conversation. We often say, "I've changed my mind," yet we seldom say, "I've changed my heart." The mind is capable of being quickly reprogrammed, while the heart isn't. To carry out the spacecraft analogy, we could say the heart is the wired circuit of our personal guidance system, while the mind is like the random access memory (RAM) of a computer chip, quickly changed and reprogrammed.

This distinction between heart and mind appears throughout the Bible. Scripture suggests that our hearts guide what our minds think, so an evil heart can direct the mind to devise evil schemes. Notice how the Bible describes the human race just before the Flood:

> The LORD saw how great the wickedness of the human race had become on the earth, and that every inclination of the thoughts of the human heart was only evil all the time (Gen 6:5).

Fallen humanity had turned against God and did not want to serve him. Note that Scripture says, "Every inclination...of the human heart was only evil all the time." Evil thinking bubbled up from each individual's evil heart. Now notice how the psalmist described a wicked person:

> Rescue me, Lord, from evildoers;
>   protect me from the violent,
> who devise evil plans in their hearts
>   and stir up war every day (Ps 140:1-2).

The psalmist knew that every ungodly person has the same basic problem—"heart disease." When a person's heart is not right, their life purpose is not right. As the King James puts it, such a person "imagines mischiefs" continually. When a mischievous heart steers a person, every decision and plan springs from its malevolent purpose.

We cannot expect that we will act differently until God changes the goal-setting center of our lives, and he can do that. He can give every one of us a new character and a new vision of our future. The Old Testament man named Saul was a case in point. He was the son of a farmer, who sent him out one day to look for some stray donkeys. Saul searched and searched without success and finally decided to consult the prophet Samuel, hoping he might know where the donkeys were. However, the prophet discerned that God wanted this young man to lead the Israelites in battle against their enemies, the Philistines. He announced that Saul's donkey-rustling days were over—he was a soldier now!

> Saul answered, "But am I not a Benjamite,
> from the smallest tribe of Israel, and is not my

clan the least of all the clans of the tribe of Benjamin? Why do you say such a thing to me?" (1 Sam 9:21).

The prophet was undeterred. He knew God's purpose for Saul, so he predicted that God would give him several signs to prove he should take this new assignment.

First, Saul would meet two friends of his father who would tell him to get along home. (Interesting! We tend to think that when God gives us new goals, he shuts the door to old opportunities. That wasn't so for Saul.)

Second, Saul would meet strangers who would give him bread without his asking. (We often think that when God calls us to do something, he will make us scrounge and scrimp for the means to do it. But that wasn't so for Saul.)

Third, Saul would meet a band of prophets singing, dancing, and prophesying as they traveled down the road. This was the strangest sign of all, for Samuel said,

> The Spirit of the LORD will come powerfully upon you, and you will prophesy with them; and you will be changed into a different person (1 Sam 10:6).

We often think that when God gives us new goals in life, he changes only our goals. But when the Spirit of God came upon Saul, he became "a different person." The shy, quiet farm boy turned into a whirling, singing prophet. So Saul's third sign of a God-given change in goals was a change in his personality. All three signs came soon after Saul left the prophet's house, proving

## Are You Setting Goals or Just Making Plans?  15

that God was calling him to be the captain of Israel. Notice verse 9:

> As Saul turned to leave Samuel, *God changed Saul's heart*, and all these signs were fulfilled that day (italics mine).

Saul acted differently because God changed the very core of his life. He changed Saul's decisions and actions by changing his "heart," the seat of his goals and aspirations.

Unfortunately, years later, Saul's heart changed again. He usurped the high priest's authority, kept the spoils of battle, consulted the witch of Endor, and disobeyed the Lord in other ways. He became so impulsive, volatile, and vain that Samuel had to denounce him and find a new king.

Notice this: Though God had changed his internal guidance system, Saul retained control of his life. He could choose to heed the dictates of his changed heart or override them to suit more selfish purposes. Sadly, he chose to turn his heart away from God to serve and promote himself. He ignored the readings of his spiritual "instruments" and instead followed his own perverse desires. In the process, Saul wrecked his life.

There are many other Old Testament examples of how God can use a person's spiritual internal guidance system to direct goal-setting, but let's notice what the New Testament says about the heart. Jesus teaches that the "heart" guides our entire life (Matt 12:34; Mark 7:21–23; Luke 6:43–45). The heart dictates what we say; it organizes what we think; it initiates what we do; it brings forth every emotion we feel. Visualize your "heart" as the switchboard at the center of your thoughts, feelings, and actions. If you change the alignment of your heart, you change your entire life. Jesus condemned the evil things that come from the heart of an evil person, but commended the good things that come from the heart of a good person:

> A good man brings good things out of the good stored up in his heart, and an evil man brings evil things out of the evil stored up in his heart. For the mouth speaks what the heart is full of (Luke 6:45).

What accounts for the difference? Why do some people have hearts that honor the Lord, while others don't?

A person's own choice accounts for the difference. Each one of us decides whether to receive or shun God's transforming power. We decide whether to follow our rebellious heart or receive a loyal, obedient heart for God. When Gentiles began giving themselves to Jesus Christ, Peter said:

> God, who knows the heart, showed that he accepted them by giving the Holy Spirit to them, just as he did to us (Acts 15:8).

We say people "give their heart to the Lord" at the time of conversion because that is exactly what happens. A Christian convert gives the goal-setting core of life to God, allowing God to change it. The apostle Paul wrote:

> . . . God's love has been poured out into our hearts through the Holy Spirit, who has been given to us (Rom 5:5).

> But thanks be to God that, though you used to be slaves to sin, you have come to obey from your heart the pattern of teaching that has now claimed your allegiance. You have been set free from sin and have become slaves to righteousness (Rom 6:17–18).

What a dramatic change God worked in your life when you became a Christian! He began changing the very core of your life—your "heart"—so he could govern everything else you do. The love of God took control of your heart, drawing you to follow his Word. Though once you were a slave of self, you now are a "slave of righteousness." If your heart belongs to God, your thoughts, attitudes, and actions will bear this out.

The Bible reveals that every person's spiritual internal guidance system has two interrelated functions: the "heart function" (setting goals, forming your character) and the "mind function" (making daily plans to reach your goals). Just as your goals determine your plans, your heart steers your mind.[1] No matter how long or how grievously you have disobeyed God, he can transform your life by giving you a new "heart."

### *A Developing Dream: Joseph*

That transformation may not come in an instant. Your vision of the future may evolve over a period of months, even years, as God molds your heart. You may have no clear idea of your ultimate destination, seeing only the first step of change. But as you take each step (a plan), you get a better idea of where you're going (your goal).

Do you remember how this happened with the patriarch named Joseph? While a young boy, Joseph dreamed that he would become superior to all his brothers, superior even to his parents. He would become a man of such great power and influence that they would bow down to him. What bombastic dreams those seemed to be! But over the next several years, Joseph realized God's plan for his life as…

- He was sold into slavery and carried into Egypt.

- He was thrown into prison, falsely accused of molesting his master's wife.

- He lay in prison fifteen years, forgotten by a prisoner he helped to free.

Only when he was called to interpret a dream for Pharaoh did Joseph become one of the most powerful men in Egypt.

That's often how God deals with us: He gives us a snapshot of what he wants us to become. Then, step by step, he develops the details of that picture. You may have only a poorly focused, fuzzy mental snapshot of the kind of person you believe God expects you to be. Or you may have no idea at all of God's expectations for your life. You may feel like saying, "Where's the camera and how do I take that picture?"

Later in this book, we'll give you a series of questionnaires you can use as a kind of "goal camera." Before we start snapping pictures of the future, though, we need to deal with some pointed questions:

- How can you know whether your goals are truly God-given?

- How can you overcome the fear of change in order

to pursue your goals?

- How can you shake off the numbness of indecision when several goals seem right for you?
- How can you know when it's time to take another step toward your goals?

We will take up these questions in the next four chapters.

---

1. Moral psychologist Jonathan Haidt uses the analogy of a mahout riding an elephant. The elephant represents the emotional, instinctive forces that drive us (i.e., the "heart") while the mahout represents our logical, purposeful way of thinking (the "mind"). The mahout may think he's in charge, but the elephant goes where he wishes. See Jonathan Haidt, *The Righteous Mind* (New York: Vintage, 2013), 53f.

*The life you see me living is not "mine," but it is lived by faith in the Son of God, who loved me and gave himself for me. I am not going back on that.* — Galatians 2:20, THE MESSAGE

## 2. How to Test Your Goals

When prospectors went West in the 1850s to search for gold, the smart ones carried a vial of nitric acid to test the nuggets. When they picked up a piece of ore that looked like gold, they would scrape it across a dark-colored slate (the "touchstone") and drip a little acid on it. If acid dissolved the scraping, it was "fool's gold" and worthless. But if the acid did nothing to the sample, a prospector knew he had found the real thing.

We ought to give our goals the acid test, too, but our acid is the Word of God. Hebrews 4:12 says:

> For the word of God is alive and active. Sharper than any double-edged sword, it penetrates even to dividing soul and spirit, joints and marrow; it judges the thoughts and attitudes of the heart.

That is how we will use the Word of God in this chapter—to judge the intentions of your heart. The Word will reveal whether they are godly intentions. And here is the first Bible standard you can use to test your goals: *A godly goal will bring glory to God.*

A carnal person strives for his own glory and honor and fame, and may even tell the Lord so. "After all, people will be so impressed with what I've done that they'll want to be Christians, too!" But that is a lie. God's first priority is not to glorify us, but himself. Jesus told the Twelve,

> This is to my Father's glory, that you bear much fruit, showing yourselves to be my disciples (John 15:8).

God's primary purpose is to bring glory to himself, although modern Christians are loath to accept the idea. We envision God as a cosmic valet peering over a distant cloud, waiting for some opportunity to help us. Do we need a job? Some extra money to pay our bills? A cure to some dreaded illness? We'll just ask the Lord and he will give us what we want. But this attitude overlooks God's reason for helping us. You see, God prospers and protects his people so that the rest of the world will realize what a great God he is. He helps us in order to demonstrate his own nature as our gracious Sovereign, not to confirm our nature as favored subjects.

The psalmist prayed, "Since you are my rock and my fortress, for the sake of your name lead and guide me." (Ps 31:3). He often had to call on the Lord for help. Why? To save his own skin? To build a spiritual reputation for himself? To spare himself biting words of criticism? He may have wanted all these things, but they did not move him to pray. He asked everything so that observers would glorify God's name.

Ponder your goals for the future. Does each one bring glory to the Lord? Would your dream home, for example, bring honor to God? Or would it make motorists park by the curb, gaze enviously at the façade, and say, "Wow! They must be pretty successful to own a place like that!"

Consider your ideal vocation or career. Would it enable people to see that God is guiding and blessing you? Or would it cause them to praise your own knowledge and skill?

Examine your goals for your church. How well would your "dream church" glorify God? Would it really help you worship and serve the Lord? Or would it help mainly in impressing your friends?

You might say, "Wait a minute! No goals are in themselves either God-honoring or self-serving. A million-dollar home might honor the Lord or it might honor me. It all depends." And so it does. It depends on your attitude toward your goals, which brings us back to the heart.

Is your heart set on serving God, no matter what he gives you? If serving him is your deepest desire, then you will be as grateful for things that do not quite fit the modern image of success as for those things that do. Does he give you a two-bedroom apartment instead of a four-bedroom house? If your heart is right, you thank him. Does he give you one rattling station wagon instead of two sleek new sedans? You thank him. When you fully delight yourself in the Lord, you want to have whatever he grants you for doing his will.

### A Goal of Fruitfulness

The second acid test for your goals is this: *A godly goal will bear fruit for the Lord.* The hope that someday you can simply enjoy God's blessings and stop bearing fruit for him is not a godly goal. Paul wrote to his Christian friends at Thessalonica:

We hear that some among you are idle and disruptive. They are not busy; they are busy-bodies. Such people we command and urge in the Lord Jesus Christ to settle down and earn the food they eat bread (2 Thess 3:11-12).

Apparently, the church at Thessalonica had its share of pikers. So did the churches at Ephesus (1 Tim 5:13), Crete (Titus 1:10-13) and elsewhere (1 Pet 4:15-17), despite our piously embellished image of the first-century church. These people liked being spectators; they enjoyed the blessings of Christian fellowship, not to mention the food! Why should they work if they could leech what they needed from other Christians? They were fruit-eaters but not fruit-bearers. Paul's guideline for them ("Such people we command...to earn the food they eat") is not one of selfishness but fruitfulness.

God laid down a similar standard through the prophet Isaiah: "I am the LORD your God, who teaches you what is best for you, who directs you in the way you should go" (Isa 48:17). God expects us to bear fruit, in other words, by doing things that benefit people around us. While the carnal person dreams of laying up riches to take life easy, the godly person dreams of serving the Lord every day of his life. I once saw a series of drawings that brought this point home. The first frame showed an elderly woman sitting on her porch, knitting a sweater and babysitting a child. The caption read, "You never retire from caring!" The next panel showed an elderly man giving a quarter to a child who had lost his balloon. The caption read, "You never retire from sharing!" The last panel showed an older woman talking on the telephone, making notes on a pad marked *Prayer Chain*.

The caption read, "You never retire from praying." That cartoonist's message was straight from the Word of God: You and I were made for a life of fruit-bearing, and we can judge whether our goals are godly by this important test.

### *A Goal of Hope*

The Bible has many other acid tests for your goals, but let me mention just one more: *A godly goal will be built on hope instead of despair.* Many people have gloomy visions for the future. They see nothing but decline and destruction in the days ahead. They say the economy is going to collapse, the government is going to fold, terrorists are going to attack, and so on. These prognosticators of gloom have a goal of survival, nothing more.

But even when God's people are in trouble, he has hopeful goals for them. When the situation is grim, God's aim is gracious. While the Jews were being led away to bondage, for example, God said through the prophet Jeremiah that they should to settle down and prosper in Babylon because he would bring them back to their homeland.

> "When seventy years are completed for Babylon, I will come to you and fulfill my good promise to bring you back to this place. For I know the plans I have for you," declares the LORD, "plans to prosper you and not to harm you, plans to give you hope and a future" (Jer 29:10–11).

It is difficult to imagine a worse situation than the Jews had. Their nation had been overrun by pagan hordes. Every family had lost their home. The temple had been destroyed. Their king had been humiliated. So God's message of hope in the midst of the smoldering ruins must have been electrifying! Yet the Jews did not believe it. They listened to a false prophet named Shemaiah who said they should rebel against their conquerors and take the future into their own hands. Although God promised them a marvelous future, they lacked the faith to believe him.

I know of no place in Scripture where God predicts a gloomy future for his people. No matter how grave the situation, God has better things ahead for those who serve him. Search the Scriptures if you think I'm exaggerating; see whether God's promises are gloomy or glorious. The apostle Paul says:

> ...Those who are led by the Spirit of God are the children of God. The Spirit you received does not make you slaves, so that you live in fear again; rather, the Spirit you received brought about your adoption to sonship. And by him we cry, "Abba, Father." The Spirit himself testifies with our spirit that we are God's children. Now if we are children, then we are heirs—heirs of God and co-heirs with Christ, if indeed we share in his sufferings in order that we may also share in his glory (Rom 8:14–17).

As children of God, we are heirs of all that He possesses. At the same time, we are called to become all that God's own children are meant to be. How's that for a life goal?

You may freeze with fear at the prospect of attempting to reach such a goal, and you may get cold feet before taking the first step, much less the steps beyond. Does the Bible offer any assurances that you can? In the next chapter, we're going to deal with the fear of becoming a different person—the person God is calling you to be.

Remember the three acid tests that you can apply to your goals to make sure they come from God:

1. Do they bring glory to God?
2. Do they bear fruit for God?
3. Are they built on hope instead of despair?

If your goals stand up to these tests, follow them, no matter how grand or incredible they seem to be. As the old prospectors learned, some things that glitter really *are* gold!

*Go ahead and build your castles in the air. That's where they belong. Now put some foundations under them.*
                                            —Henry David Thoreau

# 3. You *Can* Get There from Here

Grandfather Mountain is a beautiful landmark on the western edge of North Carolina where Dad and Mom often took our family. The mountain got its name from two craggy towers of rock whose weathered profile looks like the face of a reclining old man.

A wooden footbridge connects the two peaks, so tourists can park and cross the wobbly bridge of the Grandfather. My parents loved to do that. I didn't. Something about those creaking cables and undulating planks made my stomach queasy. I watched dozens of people stride cheerfully across the bridge—even toddlers who held onto their mothers' hands. My younger brother and sister crossed the bridge and waved from the distant rock, but I never crossed. I was too scared.

Do you ever feel that way about your life's goals? Do you hesitate to take the first step because you're not sure whether you can reach your destination? If so, let me share a secret: A Christian can reach any God-given goal if he stops asking, "What am I able to do?"

Christians who lift their eyes to distant goals are apt to ask that question. They express a fear of any new, untried way of life that God calls them to walk. That fear can paralyze and prevent them from taking even one step toward their goals. They feel as queasy as I did facing the bridge at Grandfather Mountain! Perhaps you have that fear right now. Though we have not yet examined your life goals in detail, the very idea of becoming a different kind of person may be so unnerving that you would prefer to keep your feet firmly planted where you are. But the Bible extends several promises to you as a goal-oriented Christian, assuring you that you *can* get there from here:

### Promise #1: God Knows the Way

You may not see how you could ever fulfill your goals, but God knows how you can. He has known from the beginning. The psalmist wrote,

> When my bones were being formed, carefully put together in my mother's womb, when I was growing there in secret, you knew that I was there—you saw me before I was born. The days allotted to me had all been recorded in your book, before any of them ever began (Ps 139:15-16 TEV).

Think about that for a moment: God saw you and me from the very moment we were conceived, and he knew what our days would be. His purpose for our lives was laid before we were born. We may stumble into situations that seem to defeat the goals he has given us, but since his goals for us are perfect, then they must be attainable.

Almost every Christian has heard the story of Joni Eareckson Tada, who became paralyzed at age sixteen in a swimming accident. Many looked at Joni with pity, since she "could have done" so much with her life. Yet Joni has done much. She learned to draw by holding a pencil between her teeth. She's recorded several albums.

She's begun a daily Christian radio program. She even has a new international ministry! Through all of these channels, she spreads the good news of Jesus Christ.

Joni and countless other Christians have proved Job's declaration of faith, "I know that you can do all things; no purpose of yours can be thwarted" (Job 42:2). Not one of God's purposes for you can be thwarted, either. Not by accident. Not by willful neglect. Not by anything. Your circumstances can never thwart God's ultimate purpose for your life.

But you can refuse to accept it. And there is a vast difference between following God's purpose or trying to buck it every step of the way—a vast difference in the satisfaction and the victory you find, not to mention in the sort of person you become.

Leslie Weatherhead, longtime pastor of City Temple in London, once said that the will of God is like a mountain stream: It is so small near its source that children can easily divert it with twigs and pebbles, yet gravity pulls other little branches into the stream as it flows down the mountainside until it becomes a river. Then it can be delayed by huge hydroelectric dams, but it still cannot be stopped. It moves inexorably to the sea.

Likewise, we may divert or delay the fulfillment of God's will, but we cannot destroy it. We can resist his claim upon our lives, but we cannot dismiss it. He calls us patiently toward the purpose he designed for us, and we are much happier when we understand that purpose and make it our own.

### Promise #2: God Reveals the Way

You may be reluctant to contemplate God's purpose for your life because you don't see how you can attain it, but Scripture says God will enable you to become any kind of person he wants you to become. Proverbs 16:3 promises:

> Commit to the Lord whatever you do,
>   and he will establish your plans.

This means we don't need to see every turn of life's maze before we step into it. We only need to trust the Guide who is leading us through. Though perplexing at first, the maze can even give us better understanding and maturity.

Archaeologists have unearthed an odd-looking hill in England. They thought at first it was a temple mound where Druids worshiped the sun, but they have found so many medieval artifacts that they now think it was a maze constructed by King Arthur as a testing ground for prospective knights. Atop the hill was a stone tower surrounded by a labyrinth of hedges. A young man had to negotiate the thick maze of bushes in an allotted time. Then he had to brandish his sword against guards at the base of the tower, fight his way up the stairwell and claim a prize at the top. (A bag of gold? A beautiful girl? Your guess is as good as mine.) The medieval ballads of England and France say that Merlin, the king's magician, divulged the route to lads he favored for the king's court. Only the fellows who got Merlin's help were able to reach the tower—and then they were on their own!

The way to your life goals may seem as perplexing as King Arthur's maze. You may feel mystified. But God has a way for you to reach the prize, and he will reveal that way to you as you step out. When you commit your works to the Lord, he will establish your plans.

***Promise #3: God Provides the Ability***

In an age when some people put themselves down or make light of their own abilities, the church has abetted this crime. One minister says, "I've got to get a man lost before I can get him saved." Too much Christian preaching and teaching has made unbelievers feel hopelessly lost, and convinced believers that they are teetering on the brink of failure. Some pastors convey much good news about Christ but little good news about humanity. To be sure, the Bible recognizes human sin, immaturity, and limitation. But it also shows we can rise above these things through the power of Christ. This is part of the gospel message that we need to hear more. Paul's Christian friends in Corinth, for example, were discouraged. False teachers were wrecking the church. Hedonistic culture in the city was drawing young people away from Christ. Church leaders practiced adultery and incest openly. Yet Paul began his letter to the Corinthians with this reminder:

> Brothers and sisters, think of what you were when you were called. Not many of you were wise by human standards; not many were influential; not many were of noble birth. But God chose the foolish things of the world to shame the wise; God chose the weak things of the world to shame the strong. God chose the lowly things of this world and the despised things—and the things that are not—to nullify the things that are, so that no one may boast before him. (1 Cor 1:26-29).

The Corinthian Christians were foolish, weak, base and despised, yet God chose them anyway! They lived, not in their power, but in his. That was the real measure of their ability.

In a later letter to his friends at Corinth, Paul confessed his own imperfections. In fact, he admitted a glaring imperfection that he called his "thorn in the flesh." But notice what he told the Corinthians about it:

> Three times I pleaded with the Lord to take it away from me. But he said to me, "My grace is sufficient for you, for my power is made perfect in weakness." Therefore I will boast all the more gladly about my weaknesses, so that Christ's power may rest on me (2 Cor 12:8-9).

Think of it: The mighty power of God is best seen in a weak, imperfect, incapable life. This is not to say that a Christian should remain weak or imperfect! It means that God can take your life, inadequate though it seems, and mold it to his purpose. Although Paul felt a notable flaw in A.D. 60, we have no idea what it was, and we certainly don't think it hindered his mission.

Nothing is wasted in the Kingdom of God. Even the character traits that seem weak or cumbersome to us can be reclaimed and used to God's glory. When we lived in Nashville, we drove past a huge scrap yard on our way to church—a mountain of rusty auto parts and bathtubs. The owners of that scrap yard crushed the salvage metal into tight, heavy bales, then loaded them onto flatcars for the steel mills in Birmingham, Alabama. There the scrap would be melted in white-hot furnaces to become ingots of pure metal once again. I began to think of the scrap yard as my signpost to the church. Why not? The church is where God takes rusty, bent, and broken lives and recycles them to suit his purpose. By ourselves we are nothing, but by his redeeming power we become sufficient to every task.

Think about your life goals once again. Don't consider your lack of ability, your weakness, or your fear. Consider the God who chose you to be his. Consider the unlimited power of the One who ignited such brilliant dreams in your heart. Think about the life-changing grace of the God who calls you to become his man or woman.

You will begin to realize you *can* get there from here!

*Salvation is free—"Jesus Paid It All."*
*But the life of salvation is costly—"I Surrender All."*

## 4. Building a Life Will Cost You Plenty!

A young woman named Eugenia Price worked in Chicago in the 1940s as a radio scriptwriter. She received a generous salary and lived in a posh apartment, but she felt empty. One weekend, visiting her parents in West Virginia, she met a high school friend named Ellen whom she had not seen for years. As they talked together, Eugenia perceived a radical difference in their lives. Although both had had a brash, arrogant attitude in high school, now Ellen had a quiet confidence, a radiant joy that fascinated Eugenia.

The trim businesswoman from Chicago asked her friend why she had changed. Ellen said it was because she had surrendered her life to Jesus Christ, and she urged Eugenia to do the same.

Over the next several months, Ellen corresponded with Eugenia and pressed her to become a Christian. Finally, Eugenia could stand the pressure no more. She bought a train ticket to New York City, where Ellen worked in a soup kitchen run by an Episcopal church. She spent a full week with her, learning more about the Christian way of life. Ellen kept saying, "Genie, if you're going to serve the Lord, you've got to serve him one hundred percent. You've got to give him everything."

## Building a Life Will Cost You Plenty!

As Eugenia was packing for the train trip back to Chicago, Ellen stopped by for a visit. Eugenia fussed with a cigarette as she told Ellen she was going to give Christianity a try. "I really think you're far too radical about it," Eugenia laughed. "You say I'll have to give myself up entirely, and I think that's emotionalism on your part. Or dramatics." She had concluded that the Christian life could be enormous fun, and that Jesus didn't really require so much from her.

Ellen stood up from the couch, her eyes glinting with fire. "I didn't say that. Christ said it. It isn't my idea to give yourself up entirely. It's his."

The fact was, giving Christ everything didn't square with what Eugenia had learned about making a life for herself. She thought she had to carve her own niche in the world and make her own career openings. So why give it all to Jesus? What if he decided to demolish the life she had made for herself and begin again with a different set of blueprints?

"Your interpretation is wrong," Eugenia sneered. "Extreme. Radical. God can adapt himself to me more easily than I can adapt to him!"

Gravely, Ellen picked up her coat to go. But before she did, she stepped over to Eugenia, so close that the electricity of the moment sparked between them.

"It won't work any other way," Ellen said. "Jesus says he is the way, the truth and the life; no man comes to the Father but by him. He also says that if we try to save our lives, we'll lose them. But if we lose them for his sake we'll find them."

Eugenia sank down in a plush chair by the window. "Oh God, I wish I were dead!" she moaned.

"So do I," Ellen said.

Eugenia gasped.

"The most wonderful thing would be for the old Genie Price to die right now," continued Ellen, "so a new one could be born."

The headstrong writer from Chicago gazed out the window for a long moment. Her tears stopped flowing. With an uneasy smile she turned back to her friend. "O.K," she said. "I guess you're right."[1]

The bottom line for Eugenia Price was a total commitment to Christ. That was the only way she could start building a new life for God.

It's the only way anyone can start.

Let's take a look, then, at what Jesus says about self-surrender. Let's try to understand how much he will require if you follow him in pursuit of your life's goals. Jesus addressed this point specifically to a large crowd that was following him:

> "If anyone comes to me and does not hate father and mother, wife and children, brothers and sisters—yes, even their own life—such a person cannot be my disciple. And whoever does not carry their cross and follow me cannot be my disciple" (Luke 14:26–27).

Many people then wanted to follow Jesus. Whenever people see who Jesus really is, they want to follow him. Many thousands have knelt at an altar and yearned for the wonderful changes he could bring to their lives. Many have promised to obey him because they saw a marvelous transformation in the lives of others who obeyed him.

Unfortunately, we saw the tragic consequences of self-centered discipleship during the 1970s, a time that many sociologists called the "Me Decade" because people placed a premium on personal gratification. Throngs of people claimed to be born again because it felt good to be cleansed of guilt and sin and to belong to a supportive group of other born-again people. Yet Christ soon confronts us with the cost of following him. The feeling-oriented disciples of the '70s followed Jesus as long as it felt good, but eventually they learned that the Christian life isn't always warm and cozy. Sacrifice, self-denial, suffering—these are also part of the Christian life. And many exuberant Christians turn away from Christ when the good feelings ebb away.

Jesus knew this would happen with the people who gladly listened to his parables of the Kingdom, so he warned them of the high cost of following him. He warns you and me as well. Before we commit ourselves to specific goals God has for our lives, we must be sure to count the cost of fulfilling them.

*Holy Hate*

When Jesus said that anyone who came to him had to hate his father and mother and wife and children and brothers and sisters—even his own life— he did not use the word *hate* as we usually do. When you or I say we "hate" something, we mean that we want to put it away from us; we reject it. Surely, Jesus did not mean here for us to reject our families. That would contradict everything else Jesus taught about the family. He used the word *hate* to imply that we be willing to let these things go. Love embraces while hate releases. So Jesus said we should *hate* each of these relationships, I believe he meant the opposite of being attached to them.

We might paraphrase Jesus' statement like this: "If anyone comes to me and is not willing to let go of his family...even his own life, he cannot be my disciple."

Such a price is higher than some people are willing to pay. They think there might be an easier way to be happy, a less demanding discipline that would please God, a more flexible commitment to make. So they shop around. They try substitute gospels. They experiment with religious-sounding forms of pop psychology. But nothing can take the place of full commitment to Jesus Christ. Nothing else can raise us to full stature before God. Nothing else can make us children of God and eternal heirs with Christ. Only in the red-hot crucible of commitment can we discover the refined gold of God's blessing.

Other people think, "Why count the cost of following Jesus? Why not toss caution to the winds and commit my life to him?" That approach sounds noble until God asks them for something they never expected to give. Then they are forced to take stock of their commitment. In the broiling heat of crisis, they wonder whether they should have given Christ a blank check with their lives. It seems he wants to draw too much from their account, and they wonder if they were a bit too hasty.

That is why Jesus warned us to count the cost of discipleship at the outset. Before the demands come, before our commitment is tested, before he drafts our blank check, we should consider how much we are willing to give him in the line of duty. To help us do this, Jesus told two parables.

First, he described a stonemason who planned to build a tower. "Suppose one of you wants to build a tower. Won't you first sit down and estimate the cost to see if you have enough money to complete it?" (Luke 14:28).

Unfortunately, not everyone does this. I have passed what was supposed to be a motel near the town of Marion, Indiana. I am sure the developers envisioned it to be a beautiful facility. The cinderblocks are in place. Some of the plumbing is installed. Even some brickwork was started. But the developers ran out of money and couldn't finish the job. So travelers pass the half-built shell and wag their heads in dismay. What a waste of resources! A builder should carefully count his costs before he starts to build, and so should a disciple of Jesus.

The second parable Jesus told was about a king: "Suppose a king is about to go to war against another king. Won't he first sit down and consider whether he is able with ten thousand men to oppose the one coming against him with twenty thousand?" (Luke 14:31). A commander should know how many troops are at his command as well as how many the adversary has. Yet how often human pride overrides this simple logic!

A tragic military miscalculation brought on the Falkland Islands crisis in 1982. The generals of Argentina had fewer soldiers, boats, and planes than Great Britain; yet they assumed the British would not try to defend this frigid island outpost, so they sent a landing party to stake their claim on the Falklands. They ran the risk of confrontation and they lost. Hundreds of lives were lost in the sinking of an Argentinian battleship because the generals failed to count the cost realistically.

Likewise, no Christian should dare tangle with the enemy of his soul until he has counted the cost of arming himself. The Bible says our enemy "prowls around like a roaring lion looking for someone to devour" (1 Pet 5:8). We may be destroyed if we charge into the battle unprepared!

These two word pictures from Jesus remind us of how important it is to count the cost of discipleship. This is not a trivial exercise. We must know how much we are willing to lay on the line for his sake before it is required of us.

### *The Bottom Line*

Accountants like to talk about the "bottom line" of a balance sheet. After all their mathematical turns, it comes down to this: Did we break even? Were we able to meet our expenses? Jesus tallies the "bottom line" of a Christian's commitment in clear, concrete terms. He says we must be willing to lose our family, possessions, even our life if we intend to be his disciple.

How much will it cost you to serve the Lord? Everything! You can't become God's man or woman by investing ten percent of what you have, or fifty percent, or even eighty percent. Someday he will ask you for the rest. "Those of you who do not give up everything you have cannot be my disciples" (Luke 14:33). That could mean one of two things. It could mean that God will take everything from you. (Sometimes he does that, removing money, property, family or even health to help you fulfill the mission he gives you.) It could mean, on the other hand, that he will leave everything in your possession and expect you to use all of it for his purposes. More often God works this way, calling you to manage what you have for his glory.

## Building a Life Will Cost You Plenty!

Joyce Landorf was a talented Christian singer and much-sought lecturer for women's groups. She traveled widely in her native state of California until a rare physical disorder attacked the hinge of her jaw so that she felt extreme pain whenever she spoke. Her physician recommended complete rest.

Joyce sat at home in self-pity while her husband continued his fine ministry at a Christian college. What could she do? God seemed to have taken away her only ability for serving him. It didn't seem fair! But Joyce learned much about God in those months of silence. She learned that her voice really did belong to God. She had stated this blithely before dozens of audiences, but now she knew firsthand that it was true. Her voice was his to use—or remove. During that painful convalescence, she felt the full impact of Psalm 46:10: "Be still, and know that I am God..."

Joyce Landorf eventually was able to speak and sing in public again, but during her months of silence she learned to write Christian articles and books. While one gift was "on hold," she learned to use another.

One of the first books Joyce wrote was entitled, *The High Cost of Growing*.[2] Sooner or later, every Christian learns the high cost of serving God. Jesus said we should count the cost because building a life will cost us plenty—that is to say, everything—but compare that cost to the privilege of serving him.

---

1. Eugenia Price, *The Burden Is Light!* (Old Tappan, N.J.: Spire Books, 1966), chapter 17.

2. Joyce Landorf, *The High Cost of Growing* (Nashville: Thomas Nelson, 1978). Reissued in 1983 under the title, *I'm Still Growing*.

*Modern symbols of achievement: a stopwatch, a runner, a tape.*
*Jesus' symbols of achievement: a seed, a grain stalk, a bread loaf.*
*(See Mark 4:26–29; Matt. 13:33)*

## 5. Are You on Schedule?

Punctuality was essential in the days of steam railroading, yet Littleburg's train was always late. Only one train rumbled into town each day, but the exasperated passengers waiting on the platform knew it would be at least a half-hour late, maybe more.

One bright autumn afternoon, the stationmaster noticed the locomotive's plume of black smoke in the distance. He checked his clock. How could it be? The train was on time today! He grabbed the phone, dialed City Hall, and told them the astonishing news. In moments, the mayor came roaring up to the station in a police car. The school bell rang and children poured out into the street to welcome the train. This was a historic day! At last Littleburg's train was on schedule.

As the engine ground to a halt and the mayor straightened his tie, ready to make a speech, the engineer peered out of the cab. "What's all the fuss?" he asked.

"Surely you know!" the mayor laughed. "We've come to congratulate you for bringing in the train on time!"

The engineer swallowed hard. "Well, I hate to disappoint you folks," he said, "but this is yesterday's train!"

Schedules. We grumble because of them. We say we hate them. But we Americans are notorious clock-

## Are You on Schedule?

watchers and calendar-markers, which is not altogether bad! Schedules help us accomplish things we really want to do. The schedule at your shop or office allows you to work at definite, regular hours and still have time for personal activities. The bus schedule allows children to have dependable transportation to school. The garbage pick-up schedule allows you to set those bulging plastic bags at your curb on a given night and know they will be gone in the morning. Complain about them if you wish, but your life would be more frustrating without schedules than with them.

Most of us seem to have a sense of timing in the vocational decisions we make, too. We use phrases like these:

- "I knew the time was right to...."
- "I had arrived at the stage of life when...."
- "God showed me I was ready to...."

I hear a sense of timing in our comments about the reasons for abandoning certain vocations, too. We say:

- "I wasn't moving fast enough."
- "It was a dead-end job."
- "I should have been much farther along."

Obviously, we set goals with a sense of timing and scheduling, as well as purpose and destination. But do we know God's schedule? Does God indeed have a schedule? Or are we just following a subconscious sense of timing, instilled by our culture and upbringing?

### The Schedule for Jesus' Life

To get a handle on these questions, let's take a look at Jesus' references to timing in his own earthly life. The four Gospels indicate that Jesus was following a divine schedule in his ministry.

For example, John says that in the second year of Jesus' public ministry "he did not want to go about in Judea because the Jewish leaders there were looking for a way to kill him." (John 7:1). Jesus told his disciples to go up to Jerusalem to celebrate the Passover without him. When his brothers (that is, half-brothers born to Jesus' mother, Mary) goaded him to make a public display of his divine powers, Jesus still refused. Pay careful attention to his reply:

> "My time is not yet here; for you any time will do. The world cannot hate you, but it hates me because I testify that its works are evil. You go to the festival. I am not going up to this festival, because my time has not yet fully come" (John 7:6–8).

John records that after his half-brothers left, the Lord did go to Jerusalem secretly. So why did Jesus say his time was "not yet fully come" to attend the Passover? Apparently, he meant that the time was not right for him to enter the city publicly as the Messiah, thereby forcing the Jewish leaders to deal with him.

He also went back to Jerusalem to celebrate Passover the next year. But on that occasion, he said, "The hour has come for the Son of Man to be glorified" (John 12:23). This time Jesus entered the city publicly with a great deal of fanfare, receiving the glorification of mankind. But he also died on the cross and his heavenly Father raised him from the dead; so he received the glorification of God as well.

Jesus knew he would force a confrontation with the Jewish leaders when he entered Jerusalem with his relatives, friends, and admirers cheering him on. This may be why he stated in John 7 that his time was "not yet here." But in John 12, when he declared, "The hour has come," he entered the city publicly and faced the consequences.

It is interesting, in light of Jesus' keen awareness of timing, that he could chafe at schedules, too. His goals were to be the compassionate Teacher, crucified Messiah, and risen Lord. But in the last days of his ministry, Jesus sounded almost impatient to accomplish these goals:

> "I have come to bring fire on the earth, and how I wish it were already kindled! But I have a baptism to undergo, and what constraint I am under until it is completed!" (Luke 12:49-50)

I find two vital insights here: First, Jesus sensed God had a schedule for his life, and second, Jesus measured his schedule in fulfilled time.

### Two Ways to Measure Time

All of us know how to measure elapsed time. When we glance at a wristwatch or check the calendar on our desktop computer, we note the passing of time. We assume that every day is like every other day in this respect. This kind of time measurement is so neat, orderly, and predictable that we tend to think of it as the only way to measure time.

But there is another way. The Bible calls it fulfilled time. The New Testament says that God acts in "the fullness of time" to accomplish every facet of his will (e.g., Rom 11:25; Gal 4:4; Eph 1:10). This may help to explain why Jesus would not give his disciples an exact date for his return. He said that "of that day and hour no one knows, not even the angels of heaven, nor the Son" (Mt 24:36). Critical life events are often measured in fulfilled time, as we saw in Jesus' experience. When he said his time to enter Jerusalem was "not yet fulfilled," he was not watching a calendar or checking a celestial datebook. He knew he should wait until conditions were right for him to enter the next phase of his ministry.

We can visualize the difference between fulfilled time and elapsed time if we imagine roasting a turkey for Thanksgiving dinner. For this purpose, we might measure the cooking time in two ways—with a clock or with a thermometer.

Suppose the wrapper on the turkey tells us to set the oven at 375 degrees and allow 45 minutes' cooking time for each pound of the turkey's weight. So we multiply the formula and set our stove timer accordingly. This is the elapsed time method. Near the end of Macy's Parade, we hear the buzzer go off, pull the roasting pan from the oven, and serve our golden brown delicacy. Perfect every time, right?

Not necessarily. Any number of factors might change the cooking time required. The turkey may not have been completely thawed. The oven may not be as hot as the control panel says it is. The pan may not be the recommended distance from the coil. When the recommended time has elapsed, our turkey might be a bit rare—or burned!—depending on any of these factors.

So a wise cook also measures the cooking time with a thermometer. She consults a cookbook that has a table of temperatures for roasting, and it says that when the temperature inside our turkey reaches a certain point it is fully cooked, regardless of how much time has elapsed. So the cook inserts a meat thermometer into the bird before popping it into the oven, and checks the gauge now and then to see when the cooking is done. This is the fulfilled-time system. When proper conditions are met, the cook knows she can turn off the oven and serve the turkey. Considering all of the factors involved, fulfilled time is a more reliable measure than elapsed time.

### *How to Know When Your Time Is "Fulfilled"*

Jesus' ministry leads us, then, to two important conclusions: First, that God has a pattern or schedule for his servants; and second, that God's servants can discern that schedule if they observe the fulfillment of God's prerequisite conditions rather than the simple passage of time.

How can you do that? How can you ensure that conditions are right for you to take the next step in fulfilling your life goals? I believe maturity is the key. When you are spiritually mature for your stage of life, you may consider taking a further step toward your goals.

Granted, the standard of maturity applies differently to different people. A mature infant will gurgle and coo, while a mature middle-school student will recite the Gettysburg Address. They are vastly different in their capabilities, yet each is mature. Here are some guidelines for measuring your own spiritual maturity:

1. *You make the most of the opportunities God gives you.* To get a picture of what this means, review Jesus' parable of the talents (Matt 25:14–30).

2. *Your life brings glory to God.* This means your life acts as a mirror, reflecting God's blessings to people who have not seen what he can do (Matt 5:14–16).

3. *You discriminate between good and evil choices.* You have learned the difference by repeatedly choosing the good (cf. Heb 5:14).

4. *You gladly receive instruction from God's Word and act upon it.* You have become "good soil" for the seed of the Word (Luke 8:4–15).

5. *You measure yourself by Christ.* He is the true model of spiritual maturity, rather than your friends or famous Christians you have read about (Eph 4:13).

6. *You think as a spiritual "adult"* (1 Cor 12:20). Psychologists have noted the following characteristics of adult cognitive behavior:

- An adult acknowledges reality. (Confronts the true facts of each situation, even when the facts are painful.)

- An adult defers satisfaction. (Willing to wait months, even years, for the things desired.)

- An adult contributes to community. (Addresses the needs of neighbors as well as personal needs.)

- An adult concedes predominance. (Knows one cannot get his own way every time.)

Is your own thinking mature in each of these respects?

## Are You on Schedule?

7. *You care for others as deeply as you care for yourself.* This may seem like a restatement of the third characteristic in the list above, but there is a vital difference: The psychologically mature person may address his neighbor's needs after his own needs are satisfied, but the spiritually mature person often deals with his neighbor's needs before his own (Phil 2:3–4).

8. *You apply what you've learned from your failures.* This is a rich concept. When you have a disheartening experience, don't write it off as a failure; consider it an experiment. Remember that an experiment never fails. It always teaches you something.

Dr. Malcolm Rigel, who taught counseling at Warner University in Lake Wales, Florida, gave me an interesting sidelight on this. We were returning from lunch one day when I said, "Mac, I appreciate the way you help people deal with their failures. When you bring up the subject in your spiritual retreats, you seem to have a much more positive attitude about it than I have."

He grinned. "Joe, the compost pile is the richest part of my garden. That's where I throw my kitchen scraps, lawn clippings, and all the manure I can find. It's a smelly, repulsive-looking thing. But the compost pile decays into rich humus that will feed my garden next spring. My failures and disappointments are like that. They trouble me. I would like to ignore them. But I've learned that failures can provide rich compost for my life if I apply what I learn from them."

What have you learned from your life experiments? How have you used the compost of your life? Your answers will indicate your level of maturity.

God does have a schedule for your life and he measures your progress by your spiritual maturity, rather than by days marked off your desk calendar. Here is a summary of those guidelines of spiritual maturity. Use it as a checklist to determine whether you are on schedule with God's will:

1. You make the most of the opportunities God has given you.

2. Your life brings glory to God.

3. You discriminate between good and evil choices.

4. You receive instruction from God's Word and act upon it.

5. You measure yourself by Christ.

6. You think as an adult.

7. You care for others as deeply as you care for yourself.

8. You apply what you have learned from your failures.

*In many areas of life, God invites us to consult our own sanctified preferences.*
—Paul E. Little[1]

# 6. A Portrait of Your Dream

Gatlinburg, Tennessee, is a tourist town at the entrance to the Great Smoky Mountains National Park with novelty shops and restaurants jammed side-by-side along its streets. While I strolled along the main street of Gatlinburg one crisp October afternoon, I found a portrait painter outside a candy shop sketching the figure of a young man from a color snapshot. Her technique taught me a lot about goal-setting as well as painting.

First, she took a broad brush and swabbed a faint tan color across the entire canvas. She marked the center point with a fine-tipped brush. The artist then outlined the dimensions and orientation of her subject. The snapshot showed him in a quarter-turn pose, but she turned him to a more dramatic profile position, using the fine-tipped brush to outline the bust of this handsome young man.

Next, she sketched the features of her subject's face. I could see the distinctive qualities of his personality begin to emerge. Every line expressed something of the young man's identity. The artist accentuated features only suggested by the photo; she reinterpreted the photo to express the character she saw in this youthful figure.

The Gatlinburg artist deftly portrayed her subject's expression. What was the young man's habitual mood? His outlook? His attitude toward life? I could sense each of these as she deepened the shadows here and there, lifted the highlights, and gave just the right touch to his eyes and mouth. She seemed to have a knack for expressing his character, which is the true genius of portrait-painting, the quality that sets a portrait apart from a photograph.

Then the sidewalk painter roughed in the background of her portrait. She surrounded the subject with things that indicated his special interests and involvements. Although the snapshot showed him in a plaid sports shirt, she clothed him in a soldier's uniform and put the Marine Corps insignia in the background. Glancing at some other canvases, I saw the portrait of another young man in which she had placed a T-square and blueprints, suggesting that he was an architect. She was able to express a great deal about her subject in the surrounding details.

My art lesson in Gatlinburg also taught me some things about setting goals for my life, things that might help you, too. A portrait painter and a goal-setter are doing essentially the same thing. A portrait painter expresses an image in her mind. When we set life goals, we tangibly express the dreams we have in mind. Our tools are different but our purpose is the same as the portrait painter's: We want to frame our mental picture so we can refer to it again and again.

### *Staining, Marking, and Outlining*

When the sidewalk painter stained and marked her canvas, she determined what the overall mood of the portrait would be. The subtle tan color gave the finished portrait a quiet, dignified atmosphere. When Leonardo da Vinci painted "The Last Supper" on a

# A Portrait of Your Dream

monastery wall in Milan, he began by painting the whole wall with a snowy white primer, so that in the finished painting the somber brown tones of Christ and the Twelve stand in sharp contrast to the bright white sky outside.

The staining and marking of the painter's canvas are like God's underlying presence in your life. His presence will determine the mood of your entire life. Your vocation, marital status, family makeup, and other things are the details of the picture; but your relationship with God determines the nature of your personal picture, now and in the future.

When you dream about your life ten years from now, how do you see your relationship with God? Here are some statements that may help you envision this relationship:

1. I will most often see God as

- a gentle Shepherd.
- a compassionate Friend.
- a wise Teacher.
- a righteous Judge.

2. I believe that my relationship with God will be

- deeper.
- as it is now.
- shallower.

3. I believe God will reveal his will to me most often through

- Scripture.
- inner guidance by the Holy Spirit.
- the counsel of godly friends.

4. I will come to worship services with an attitude of

- joy and expectancy.
- awe and wonder.
- solemnity and reverence.
- fear and hesitation.

5. I believe God will require

- no significant changes in my lifestyle.
- a few minor changes in my lifestyle.
- radical changes in my lifestyle. (Describe.)

6. I believe he will call me to work in

- a culture familiar to me.
- a culture foreign to me.

7. I believe I will share my convictions

# A Portrait of Your Dream

- only when asked.
- quietly and respectfully.
- openly and aggressively.

8. I believe he will use me in my neighborhood as a

- companion and helper.
- concerned listener.
- defender of people's rights.
- proclaimer of the truth.

9. I believe he will use me in the church to do the work of a

- deacon (who provides for people's material needs).
- priest (who listens and heals).
- ruler (who directs and instructs).
- prophet (who speaks and challenges).

10. I believe the Lord will use me most effectively by

- what I am.
- what I do.
- what I say.

11. My attitude toward his will is going to be

- cheerful acceptance.
- reluctant cooperation.
- complaining resistance.

12. When I consider God's purpose for my life, I feel

- overwhelmed.
- uneasy.
- comfortable.
- challenged.

13. When I consider who I am today, I feel

- restless, wanting to become as I once was.
- satisfied and contented.
- restless, wanting to become a new person.

### Features

The next step of the sidewalk artist's work was to sketch in the features of the young man's face. Now she began to express the personality of her subject.

I've enjoyed looking at some of the self-portraits made by the great Dutch painter, Rembrandt. I can see a change in the features of Rembrandt's face as the years went by. The relaxed, confident expression of his youth gave way to troubled, weary lines in his old age; he was

## A Portrait of Your Dream

plagued by family problems and debt, which took their toll on his character.

Imagine what your character lines will be ten or twenty years from now. What will be the distinctive marks of your personality? Here are some statements that will help you express what you see:

1. I believe I will be

- an introverted person.
- an outgoing person.

2. I believe my attitude toward strangers will be

- distrustful.
- trustful.

3. I believe my attitude toward my family will be

- loving.
- resentful.

4. I believe my view of the future will be

- confident.
- expectant.
- hopeful.
- gloomy.

5. I believe my sense of humor will be

- gentle and warm.
- rollicking and boisterous.
- sarcastic.

6. I believe I will cry

- when I feel grieved or disappointed.
- when I feel angry or sorrowful.
- when I feel ridiculed or embarrassed.
- hardly ever.

7. I will have the most difficulty controlling my

- sorrow.
- regret.
- fear.
- impulsiveness.
- anger.

*Background*

The Gatlinburg painter embellished her portraits with symbols of the subject's life. She put her subject in suitable clothes and planted him in surroundings that told us something about his identity. Background details can express the personality of a portrait subject as

# A Portrait of Your Dream

revealingly as the set of his lips or the lines on her brow. Who can forget Winslow Homer's dynamic paintings of sailors and fishermen, straining against their ship rigging as they peer out from the soggy hoods of their rain slickers? Or what would we know about the farm couple in Grant Wood's "American Gothic" without the man's bib overalls and pitchfork, the woman's apron, and the white clapboard farmhouse behind them?

Who will be the people in the background of your life ten years from now? How will you get along with them? What will be your style of living? Here are some statements to help you describe the background details of your dreams for the future:

1. I believe my co-workers will be

- searching for answers.
- confident they have all the answers.

2. When I'm in a large group of people, I will be

- a quiet spectator.
- a lively spectator.
- a quiet participant.
- a lively participant.
- the focus of attention.

3. When I become the kind of person God wants me to be, I may have trouble getting along with

- other Christians who don't believe as I do.
- uncommitted people.
- skeptics.

4. I believe that when my family sees the Lord's purpose for my life, they will

- approve and encourage me.
- approve but not give much encouragement.
- disapprove but not try to discourage me.
- disapprove and try to discourage me.

5. I think I will feel uncomfortable with

- quiet people.
- talkative people.

6. I think I will feel most comfortable with

- people who are a lot like me.
- people who are different from me.

7. I believe that other people's approval will

- mean a great deal to me.
- concern me but not guide me.

# A Portrait of Your Dream

- make no difference to me.

8. My life would be changed the most by the death of _____, for these reasons:

9. The person I am most eager to spend the future with is _____, because:

10. I believe I will have completed this level of education:
- elementary school.
- high school.
- vocational school or junior college.
- bachelor's degree.
- master's or doctor's degree.

11. I believe my annual income ten years from now will be at least $_____.

12. I believe I will be reading books on these subjects:

13. I believe I will attend meetings of civic groups, social clubs, or church groups such as these:

14. My house/condominium/apartment will be located in
- the city.

- the suburbs.
- the country.

15. I believe I will be living in

- the Northeast.
- the Midwest.
- the South.
- the West.
- elsewhere (name area of the world:)

The last few questions may seem trivial, but they will help you complete the portrait of your future self. You now have a full picture of your desires for the future. You have portrayed your goals; you have described yourself as you expect to be.

You can summarize your goals by compiling sentences with a component from each section of questions. You might say, for example, "The Lord will use me most effectively by what I do; my sense of humor will be rollicking and boisterous; and my attitude toward strangers will be trustful." Or you might say, "The Lord will use me most effectively by what I am; my co-workers will be people searching for answers; and my view of the future will be expectant."

Each time you compose a sentence like this, you get a thumbnail sketch of what you anticipate for your life. You get a statement of your goals.

# A Portrait of Your Dream

## *Testing Your Goals*

Test these goals with the same biblical standards we discussed earlier for testing dreams, then ask yourself these questions:

- Do I have any ungodly goals? In other words, do any of my goals miss the mark of what God expects from one of his children? There is nothing virtuous, for example, about a person who always resents or distrusts other people.

- Do I have any inadequate goals? Have I scaled down my God-given dream to fit my own shortcomings? You may hesitate to commit yourself to your God-given goals because you don't have the proper gift or ability, but God can provide these, as we will see.

- Do I have any outmoded goals? Am I clinging to a lifestyle that once was right for me but no longer honors the Lord?

- Are these really my goals, or am I adopting someone else's goals in order to please them?

Well-meaning relatives or friends can easily impose their goals upon you. They say, "You ought to be a cartographer like your Uncle Ed," or, "You have a knack for working with children." With countless good suggestions and helpful hints, they construct their own portraits of what they feel you ought to be. And it may be far easier to accept their ready-made dreams than to articulate your own.

Psychologist Theodore Lidz tells the story of a young man whose father expected him to become a building contractor. The father had made a lucrative business of it, so he thought his son should continue the family tradition. The son didn't like the construction business; he wanted to be a concert pianist. But to please his father, he went to trade school and acquired the necessary skills. Then he built a sprawling apartment complex in New York City and sold it at a large profit. His father was very happy until the young man took his profits and went to Europe to study piano! The young millionaire decided to pursue his own goals rather than his dad's. Lidz does not say whether the father ever forgave him; but the young man knew he could not be accountable to his father forever.[2]

To serve God, you must be accountable to him, striviing to live in a way that pleases and glorifies him. Other people will clamor for satisfaction, but if you are striving to please God, you cannot please all of them. How about it—can you give a good account of yourself to God?

Visions can be wonderful. God-given visions can become challenging goals. Let's be sure our visions and goals come from him. If we plan to build on a framework of faulty goals, we are sure to be disappointed. But if we build on goals that honor the Lord, our lives will be rewarding and satisfying.

Planning to build—that's the next step.

---

1. Paul E. Little, *Affirming the Will of God* (Downers Grove, Ill.: InterVarsity Press, 1971), 7.

2. Theodore Lidz, *The Person* (New York: Basic Books, 1976), 490.

*Any job, marriage, move, investment, or expenditure which leads us away from being a communicator of the Lord is not best for us or his purposes in our lives.* —Lloyd J. Ogilvie[1]

# 7. Becoming What You Choose

Terrence Johnston worked one of the last one-man coal-mining operations in this country. In a low, dusty tunnel shaft near Altoona, Pennsylvania, he burrowed chunks of soft coal from the earth with a pickax in the 1980s. Two Shetland ponies harnessed to an oak dump car stood obediently behind him. On a good day, they might haul two tons of coal from the tunnel. Terrence sold it to his neighbors for $25 a ton, with $10 of that going to taxes and lease rights. He lived with his wife and two daughters in a tarpaper shack at the mouth of the mine.

"It's nothing to brag about," said Terrence, "but it's good enough for me. Some people are dissatisfied with their work. Me, I'm perfectly comfortable and quite content. I'm here by choice, and I'm just as happy as if I had good sense."[2]

His comment proved he already had good sense. By affirming that he was there by choice, Terrence Johnston showed a profound insight that many philosophers never perceive. You and I got where we are by choice. We will be where we are ten years hence by choice. And so it will be forever.

God lets every person choose how he will live. God could be sovereign in all things, but he allows you and me to be sovereign in making life choices.

We choose how we will live in spite of circumstances. Circumstances limited the work of John Bunyan, the eloquent Nonconformist preacher of seventeenth-century England, when authorities jailed him and banned his preaching. But Bunyan could still choose how to live in jail; no man could take that away from him. So Bunyan wrote *Pilgrim's Progress* and other classic devotional books while sitting on the dank, musty straw of his cell. He chose how he would live in spite of his circumstances.

Grim consequences faced Chester Bitterman and other Wycliffe Bible translators in the jungles of Central America. They knew they might be captured, tortured, and killed by rebel soldiers in the area. Bitterman considered the consequences and chose to go anyway. He was kidnapped, accused of being a spy, and shot. Chet Bitterman chose how he would live in spite of the consequences.

A person also chooses how he will live in spite of coercion. Communist coercion filled the prison camps of Russia with hundreds of Christians arrested for distributing gospel literature and meeting for worship. In many cases, the Soviet government stripped these people of their jobs and confiscated their possessions in an attempt to pressure them into giving up their faith. Yet these Christians chose to evangelize their country.

No one can say they are unable to make choices. God gives every man and woman the power to choose. We may have to choose in the shadow of unfavorable circumstances or unexpected coercion; but every one of us chooses how we live our lives. A goal-oriented Christian chooses to live according to God's general will and according to the unique pattern God has established for him. These daily choices are the plans of his life.

In the first six chapters, we focused on our future vision of ourselves—our dreams—which are in essence our goals. We have articulated them. We have tested them. We have corrected them where they would dishonor the Lord or betray our integrity. Now we are ready to make plans for achieving our goals so we can become what we have chosen.

## *Examples of Goal-Oriented Plans*

Let's look at samples of plans that might be used to achieve the goals you set in Chapter 6. We'll refine these plans later. For now, I just want to give you an idea of how effective, goal-oriented plans look:

| *Goal* | *Plan* |
|---|---|
| 1. Become more spiritually mature. | 1. Spend a half-hour in prayer each morning; read a chapter of the New Testament each day. |
| 2. Become an outgoing person. | 2. Introduce myself to one stranger each day; send a friendship greeting card. |
| 3. Become a vocational-technical school graduate. | 3. Get a catalog from Ivy Tech; schedule interview with admissions director. |

There are three important features to observe in these goal-oriented plans.

First, notice that each of the goals is a "be" statement. Even #3, which seems at first to be a "do" statement, is really saying, "I will be a vocational school graduate."

Each "do" statement is a specific plan of action that moves you one step closer to becoming the person God expects you to be.

Second, notice that each plan statement is a specific plan. We are tempted to make vague, general plans so we won't have to admit failure. We might say, for example, "Oh, I *did* take more time for Bible study last week, like that morning I read the Lord's Prayer at breakfast." A vague plan cannot fail, because it allows us to define later what the plan really was. By the same token, a vague plan seldom motivates us to make significant change in our lives. If you want to reach specific life goals, you need to make specific plans.

Third, notice that the plans are only beginning steps; they will not renovate your life overnight. Always think in terms of long-range growth. You acquired your present habits, attitudes, and intentions over many years, so expect many years to change them. Allow a realistic amount of time for achieving your goals.

Counselors at weight-loss clinics say that people who set unrealistic goals or plans are usually the ones who drop out. There is the desperate high school senior, for example, who wants to shed two dress sizes before the prom. In order to lose thirty pounds by the end of the month, she goes on a crash diet of 500 calories a day. She is setting herself up for failure because the human body cannot handle such radical changes in such a short time. The same is true for any other aspect of life.

When the Bible says you can be "transformed by the renewing of your mind" (Rom 12:2), it does not mean you can be transformed as soon as you change your mind! Just as the high school senior needs to change her

## Becoming What You Choose

pattern of eating so she will lose weight in a gradual, permanent way, it takes a while to change your life. God must redirect your heart, your heart must redirect your mental outlook, and your mental outlook must redirect your actions. So be patient with yourself. As the folk philosopher Max Ehrmann wrote, "Enjoy your achievements as well as your plans."[3]

Your plans should be aimed at action, they should be specific, and they should allow realistic time for change. With these guidelines in mind, let's begin making some plans for your life based on the goals you have set.

### *Worksheet for Planning*

Here is a simple pen-and-paper exercise you can use to make plans for reaching your life goals, a method you can employ any time you believe the time is ripe for a change:

A. Compare your real self to your ideal self

Check the appropriate slot on each of the scales that follow. First, put an "X" for each of the answers you gave in Chapter 6 for your future, ideal self. Then put an "O" to show where you think you are now. Here is a sample:

1. I most often see God as
_X_ Shepherd
___ Friend
_O_ Teacher
___ Judge

This person ideally wants to see God as a gentle Shepherd (X), but right now sees him as a wise Teacher (O). The person will need to make changes in this area to become more like his ideal self. Now fill in your own X's and O's:

My Relationship with God

1. I most often see God as
    ___ Shepherd
    ___ Friend
    ___ Teacher
    ___ Judge

2. I believe my relationship with God should be
    ___ deeper
    ___ as it is
    ___ shallower

3. I believe he reveals his will to me most often through
    ___ Scripture
    ___ Spirit
    ___ godly counsel

4. I come to worship services with an attitude of
    ___ joy
    ___ awe
    ___ solemnity
    ___ fear

5. I believe God requires
    ___ no changes
    ___ few changes
    ___ radical changes in my lifestyle

6. I believe he calls me to work in
    ___ a familiar culture
    ___ a foreign culture

**Becoming What You Choose**

7. I believe I will share my convictions
    ___ when asked
    ___ quietly
    ___ openly

8. I believe God uses me in my neighborhood as a
    ___ companion
    ___ listener
    ___ defender
    ___ proclaimer

9. I believe God uses me in the church as a
    ___ deacon
    ___ priest
    ___ ruler
    ___ prophet

10. I believe God uses me most effectively by
    ___ what I am
    ___ what I do
    ___ what I say

11. My attitude toward God's will is
    ___ acceptance
    ___ cooperation
    ___ resistance

12. When I consider God's purpose for my life, I feel
    ___ overwhelmed
    ___ uneasy
    ___ comfortable
    ___ challenged

13. When I consider who I am, I feel
    ___ restless
    ___ satisfied

My Identity

1. I believe I am
    ___ introverted
    ___ outgoing

2. I believe my attitude toward strangers is
    ___ distrustful
    ___ trustful

3. I believe my attitude toward my family is
    ___ loving
    ___ resentful

4. I believe my view of the future will be
    ___ confident
    ___ expectant
    ___ hopeful
    ___ gloomy

5. My sense of humor is
    ___ gentle
    ___ rollicking
    ___ sarcastic

6. I cry when I feel
    ___ grieved
    ___ angry

## Becoming What You Choose

\_\_\_ ridiculed
\_\_\_ hardly ever

7. I have the most difficulty controlling my
   \_\_\_ sorrow
   \_\_\_ regret
   \_\_\_ fear
   \_\_\_ impulsiveness
   \_\_\_ anger

My Relationships with Others

1. I believe my co-workers are
   \_\_\_ searching for answers
   \_\_\_ confident they have the answers

2. When I'm in a large group of people, God usually expects me to be a
   \_\_\_quiet spectator
   \_\_\_lively spectator
   \_\_\_quiet participant
   \_\_\_lively participant

3. I have trouble getting along with
   \_\_\_other Christians
   \_\_\_uncommitted people
   \_\_\_skeptics

4. When my family sees God's purpose for my life, they
   \_\_\_approve and encourage
   \_\_\_approve but not encourage
   \_\_\_disapprove but not discourage
   \_\_\_disapprove and discourage

5. I feel uncomfortable with
   ___ quiet people
   ___ talkative people

6. I feel most comfortable with
   ___ people like me
   ___ people different from me

7. Other people's approval
   ___ means a great deal to me
   ___ concerns but does not guide me
   ___ often determines what I do

(Questions 8 and 9 are omitted from the scales.)

10. I have completed
    ___ elementary school
    ___ high school
    ___ vocational school or junior college
    ___ bachelor's degree
    ___ master's or doctor's degree

11. My annual income is
    ___ less than $20,000
    ___ $20,000–$44,999
    ___ $45,000–$69,999
    ___ $70,000–$99,999
    ___ $100,000+

(Questions 12 and 13 are omitted from the scales.)

14. My house/condominium/apartment is located in

___city
___suburbs
___country

15. I am living in
___the Northeast
___the Midwest
___the South
___the West
___outside the U.S.A.

B. List opportunities for change.

When you have completed the scales under Part A, you will see what areas of your life you need to change the most in order to fulfill your personal goals. Now list the areas in which you want to begin making changes and note some opportunities for change.

My Relationship with God
    Change Needed:


    Opportunity for Change:



My Identity
    Change Needed:


    Opportunity for Change:

My Relationships with Other People
Change Needed:


Opportunity for Change:



C. Consider the preparation you'll need.

You will need to make certain kinds of preparation to take advantage of each opportunity you listed under Part B. Here are four basic kinds of preparation you should consider:

*Knowledge.* What information will I need to know in order to do this?

*Insight.* What will I need to understand about God, about myself, or about others in order to do this?

*Sensitivity.* What leadings of God or feelings of other people should I be aware of?

*Conditioning.* What skills will I need to learn or develop?

I call these four kinds of preparation the K-I-S-C formula. Here is how you might use the K-I-S-C formula to prepare for one of your growth opportunities:

*Change Needed:* A deeper relationship with the Lord.

*Opportunity for Change:* Join a Tuesday night Bible study group in my neighborhood.

*Preparation I'll Need:*

KNOWLEDGE: I will contact someone who is already in the group to find out where they meet, when, who leads the group, and how to join.

INSIGHT: I will consider whether this particular Bible topic will truly help me grow. I can then observe the group and perhaps visit one of their sessions, to see whether they would truly challenge me to grow

SENSITIVITY: I will watch how the leader relates to the rest of the group, how the group members get along with each other, what their attitude is toward me as a newcomer, etc. And I will find out whether the Lord approves of my belonging to this group.

CONDITIONING: I will discipline myself to attend the meetings every Tuesday. I will also set aside an hour each day for my Bible study homework, and practice using my study Bible so I can learn how to use the cross-references and other Bible study helps in it.

As you can see, the K-I-S-C formula gives you the first steps of an action plan. Now try the K-I-S-C to begin thinking about how you can prepare for a growth opportunity in each area:

My Relationship with God
*Change Needed:*


*Opportunity for Change:*


*Preparation Needed:*

KNOWLEDGE:

INSIGHT:

*Sensitivity:*

*Conditioning:*

D. Write your action plan.

Step C gave you the preparation phase of an action plan. When you write out a full-fledged action plan, you should be able to describe your preparation (how you will get ready to do it), your implementation (how you will do it), and your evaluation (how to judge the success of what you did). Take the first growth opportunity you listed under Part B and write an action plan below.

Preparation:

(Take everything you wrote under the K-I-S-C formula and list it in sequence—what you should do first, second, third, and fourth to prepare for what you are planning to do.)

Implementation:

(Write a fuller description of the opportunity itself. Be specific. Exactly what do you plan to do? When will you begin? How long will you continue? Which personal goal will this activity help you reach?)

Evaluation:

(Describe the standards you will use to determine whether this activity is really helping you meet your goal. What specific changes do you expect to see in yourself or in others? How long should you wait before evaluating what you are doing? What would cause you to stop doing it? Again, be specific and realistic. Suppose

I said, "I'll stop if I feel I shouldn't be doing this." That would not describe what specific feelings would tell me to stop. And since all feelings are so changeable, it would be unrealistic to let my feelings tell me what I should or should not do.)

Remember, your goals are what you intend to become, while your plans are what you intend to do. Your plans grow out of your goals. To put it another way, your goals (future identity) inspire your plans (immediate course of action).

We usually look at the process from the near end, of course. Instead of thinking about whether we will be trim or obese ten years from now, we think about what we will eat for lunch today. Instead of visualizing what sort of attitude we will have toward strangers ten years from now, we elbow our way to the head of the grocery line today.

But today's impulsive actions come from the picture we have of ourselves; and when we telescope that picture a decade or so into the future and test it in light of God's Word, we begin to make intentional changes in the way we act today.

Every day we choose what we shall do; simultaneously, we choose what we shall become. The point of this book is that we can approach life the other way: We can consciously choose what we shall become, and let that guide what we choose to do.

My heart sings when I find another Christian who has made the discoveries I am making about dreams and goals. While writing this chapter I came across John Powell's book, *Fully Human, Fully Alive,* which was very popular in the 1970s. Powell writes about our "visions"—

how we picture ourselves in the present as well as the future. He calls the process of creative dreaming and goal-setting "vision therapy," and he says:

> If you or I are to change, to grow into persons who are more fully human and more fully alive, we shall certainly have to become more aware of our vision and patiently work at redressing its imbalances and eliminating its distortions. All real and permanent growth must begin here. There can be no real change, no real growth in any of us until...our vision is changed.[4]

Every brushstroke of your daily planning should portray a bit more of your God-given purpose. Each activity can sketch in another detail of the ideal self you envision. Everyday decisions can flesh out a commitment you have made to the Lord. Keep on consulting your vision of the finished portrait to make sure each decision helps to perfect it. God has given you the vision. God will lead you in defining the goals and plans that will fulfill it.

But he doesn't stop there. He also gives you the natural abilities and supernatural gifts to do all these things. Let's consider what these are.

---

1. Lloyd J. Ogilvie, *God's Will in Your Life* (Eugene, Ore.: Harvest House Publishers, 1982), 73.

2. "Lone Coal Miner Works with 2 Ponies and a Cart," *The New York Times*, December 11, 1983, 1: 44.

3. Max Ehrmann, "Desiderata," copyright 1927, 1954 by Bertha Ehrmann.

4. John Powell, *Fully Human, Fully Alive* (Allen, Tex.: Argus Communications, 1976), 14.

*Anything will give up its secrets if you love it enough.*
   —George Washington Carver

# 8. Develop Your Abilities

Queen Elizabeth I felt confident of her ability to rule the British Empire. Her keen mind unraveled the most complicated problems of state. Her discerning intuition chose leaders who ably served the Crown. Her flattering tongue reconciled the most bitter enemies of her court. She once said, "I thank God that I am endued with such qualities that if I were turned out of the Realm in my petticoat, I were able to live in any place in Christendom."[1]

You may not feel as confident of your own abilities, but you do have them, including the ability to serve God. Your future happiness depends in large measure on how well you develop your abilities, especially your service-ability. Two well-known vocational counselors at Trinity College put it this way: "Career satisfaction is in direct proportion to the extent people have opportunity to use their assets and abilities in achieving worthwhile goals."

If you walked into a vocational counselor's office and said, "Show me what my abilities are," the counselor would probably hand you a simple inventory form developed by the Department of Labor. Here it is in condensed form:

*Reasoning (Intellectual) Ability.* I am able to take instructions, make decisions and arrive at conclusions based on the information available.

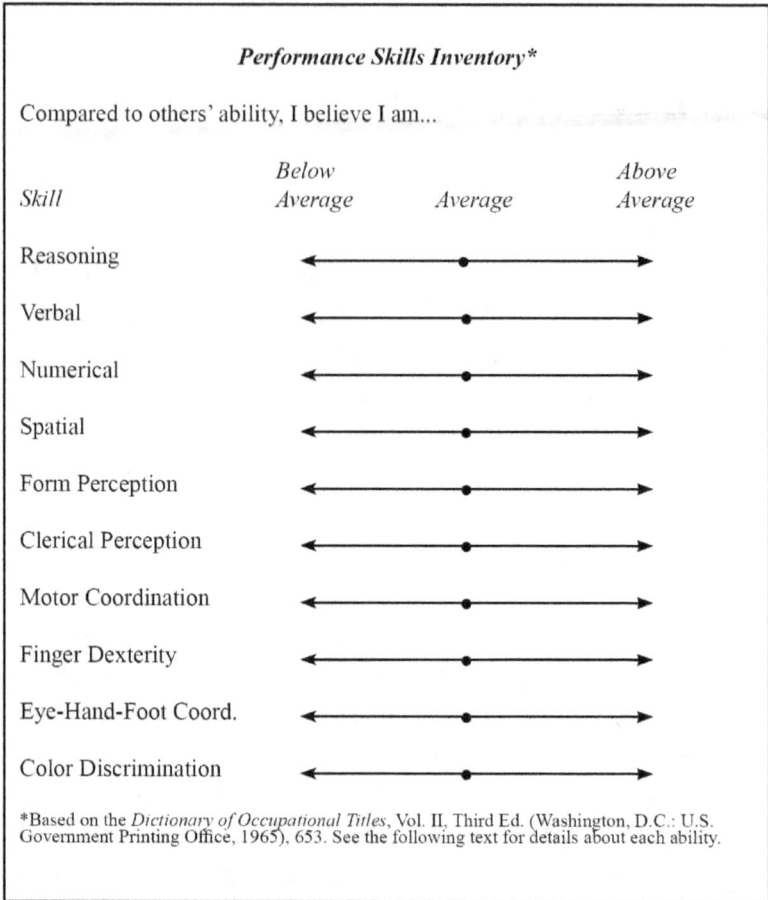

*Verbal (Reading, Speaking and Listening) Ability.* I understand what words mean and am able to communicate my ideas effectively in written or oral form.

*Numerical (Mathematical) Ability.* I can add, subtract, multiply or divide numbers quickly and accurately.

*Spatial (Sketch Interpreting) Ability.* I can understand the relationship of two or more objects on a diagram or blueprint.

## Develop Your Abilities

*Form Perception (Sorting) Ability.* I quickly see differences of size, tone or color in objects on a picture or diagram.

*Clerical Perception (Proofreading) Ability.* I quickly see errors in printed or typewritten material, and easily detect errors in arithmetic.

*Motor Coordination (Manual) Ability.* I can coordinate my hands with my eyes, performing delicate maneuvers with speed, precision and a steady hand.

*Finger Dexterity (Digital) Ability.* I can gather and assemble small objects quickly and skillfully; I can operate calculators or other small instruments swiftly and accurately.

*Eye-Hand-Foot Coordination (Steering) Ability.* I can respond quickly to what I see, using my hands and feet to operate mechanical equipment smoothly and efficiently.

*Color Discrimination (Matching) Ability.* I can recognize similarities and differences in colors, matching them or contrasting them for pleasing results.

Why are abilities important in goal-setting? Because the Lord wastes nothing. He had a purpose for your life from the moment you were conceived, so he did not endow you with abilities to ignore, suppress, or throw away. He gave you abilities that would help you fulfill his purpose.

When you visualize what sort of person God expects you to become, you find that your innate abilities are a vital part of that dream. An ability does not dictate what you should become; but like the quivering needle of a compass, it can indicate the direction you should take.

List the three areas of the Performance Skills Inventory in which you seem to have the best ability:

1.
2.
3.

The vocational counselor would use your answers to help you identify jobs that would call up your best abilities, whether in gardening, manufacturing, clerical work, managerial work or hundreds of other career areas. You can do the same.

In fact, you have already started. When you pictured your goals for the future, you began thinking about your abilities. When you made plans to reach your goals, you subconsciously took stock of your abilities. Though you may not have pondered it in these terms, God calls you to a future that employs your best abilities.

Look back at the personal goals you outlined in Chapter 6 and the plans you made for achieving these goals in Chapter 7. I believe that if they are truly Christ-honoring goals and plans, they will maximize your abilities, not muffle them. Here are some occupations that may be well-suited to you if you are above average in:

*Reasoning Ability.* Journalism and creative writing, music, scientific research, medicine, engineering, sales, social casework and counseling, mathematics and statistics, teaching, library science, business administration, law.

*Verbal Ability.* Journalism and creative writing, drama, music, scientific research, medicine, engineering, sales, managerial work, social casework and counseling, mathematics and statistics, teaching, library science, business administration, law, law enforcement.

*Numerical Ability.* Medicine, engineering, mathematics and statistics, law, finance.

### Develop Your Abilities

*Spatial Perception.* Art, scientific research, medicine, engineering, piloting, equipment operation, mathematics and statistics, athletics.

*Form Perception.* Fine arts, scientific research, medicine.

*Clerical Perception.* Clerical work, sales, hospitality, nursing, mathematics and statistics.

*Motor Coordination.* Art, music, laboratory technology, barber and beauty services, crafts, athletics.

*Finger Dexterity.* Art, music, medicine, industrial production, crafts, athletics.

*Manual Dexterity.* Music, laboratory technology, agriculture, engineering, industrial production, clerical work, customer services, athletics.

*Eye-Hand-Foot Coordination.* Music, dancing, law enforcement, piloting, equipment operation, athletics.

*Color Discrimination.* Drama, barber and beauty services, interior decorating, fashion design, nursing.

### A Universal Ability

God gives every person the ability to serve him. When Scottish church leaders drew up the Westminster Shorter Catechism to train young Christians in the basic tenets of their faith, they asked, "What is the chief end of man?" Students were taught to say, "The chief end of man is to glorify God and enjoy him forever." In other words, every human being's life purpose revolves around God. We were made to reflect his design. Our deepest satisfaction is knowing that God accepts us, loves us, and lives within us.

When the Father, Son, and Holy Spirit consulted together to create the first man and woman, they said, "Let us make mankind in our image, in our likeness..."

(Gen 1:26). God made everything else according to patterns he devised for the created order, but he made mankind according to a unique pattern. Only human beings have the image of God himself in their souls, which is ready to be expressed in every person's life. Every woman and man has the innate ability to reflect God's own nature.

Even when our lives have been wrecked by sin or misfortune, we still have the image of God within. Any person can become a child of God by responding to God's revelation of himself in Christ Jesus (John 1:12). *Any person can!* That's the glorious good news of salvation.

A Christian is a person who chooses to flesh out the image of God within him. He patterns his life after the character of God. He has "since you have taken off your old self with its practices and have put on the new self, which is being renewed in knowledge in the image of its Creator (Col 3:9b–10). While every person has the ability to serve God, a Christian intentionally does it. Thus, the Christian develops service-ability.

As you exercise your ability to serve God, you become better able to serve. One point from Jesus' parable of the talents (Matt 25:14–30) illustrates this beautifully. The manager in that parable gave his servants a supply of resources to be invested on his behalf, each according to his own ability. The servants with better managerial ability got more resources to manage. This, said Jesus, is how the Kingdom of heaven operates, too.

It seems fair enough for the man in Jesus' story to do this, but grossly unfair for God. After all, God gave us our abilities in the first place, including our service-ability; and if some people are better able to serve and

## Develop Your Abilities

glorify God, isn't it only because God gave them that extra measure of service-ability? Doesn't God determine who will be more adept at serving?

No. God enables each of us to serve him, but he does not determine which of us will become more adept at it. We determine that ourselves. Some of us become more adept at serving God because we exercise our ability to serve him. Even in this parable, the landowner chose men who proved they were able to serve. And to the ones who had proven their ability more than others, he gave greater responsibilities and more resources.

### How to Develop Your Service-Ability

The ability to serve God is the chief ability to develop as a Christian disciple, regardless of your aims in life. You can do it by employing each of the three aspects of service-ability: availability, dependability, and accountability.

First, employ your *availability*. Army veterans are fond of saying, "Never volunteer for anything; you're bound to get hard duty." (They learn that lesson when they step forward for "sit-down duty" and get a potato peeler!) But a servant in the Kingdom of God is happy to volunteer. Gladly say yes when the Master calls you to do something, even something as tedious as peeling potatoes. Jesus may call at any time because the servant is available. Are you worried about being able to do what God calls you to do? Then use your availability, and watch how he adds other abilities to your life!

Second, employ your *dependability*. Prove to the Lord that you will carry out your assignments. Show other people that they can lean on you. This is one of the most critical components of your ability to serve.

Several years back, I was working as an editor at a religious publishing house. We had tight deadline schedules to meet and I sometimes had to call freelance writers to pick up assignments that other people had dropped. I kept the names and phone numbers of my most dependable writers in a little red book inside my shirt pocket. When a deadline stared at me from the calendar and my material had not arrived on time, I would whip out the address book and call my dependable people. I knew they would bail me out. Those were the writers I called to do the more substantial jobs, too. They had proven the quality of their work and the punctuality of their service. It made good business sense to call on dependable people.

It makes good sense in the Kingdom of God, too. As we saw in Jesus' parable, the people who prove their service will be asked for more service. When God knows he can count on you, he gives you more responsibility.

Finally, employ your accountability. Be ready to answer to God for the way you are living. Live and serve in such a way that you would never be ashamed to give him a personal report of your day's activities. You are continually accounting to someone for the way you live. You are trying to please someone. The crucial question is, Are you trying to please the Lord?

Here, then, are three ways to develop your ability to serve God: by exercising your availability, your dependability, and your accountability wherever he calls you to serve. An athlete tones up muscles by going to a health spa or gym every week to lift weights or flex the springs. Likewise, you can tone up your most

## Develop Your Abilities

basic ability as a servant to the King by exercising it. You become better able to do God's will by doing his will. You become more adept at finding God's will by following his will.

---

1. Kirk E. Farnsworth and Wendell H. Lawhead, *Life Planning* (Downers Grove, Ill.: InterVarsity Press, 1981), 50.

*If some service I am performing is helping other Christians in a significant way or bringing others to Christ, then it is quite likely I am making use of a spiritual gift.*—M. Blaine Smith[1]

## 9. Discover Your Gifts

My wife had a creative sense of playfulness. She once hosted a wedding shower where she decided to give her gift to the prospective bride in an unusual way: Instead of wrapping the present and putting it on the table with the other gifts, she hid it and gave the bride clues to where it was. The first clue directed her to the place she could find the second clue, and so on. After about half a dozen clues, she found her gift—a Mexican wall hanging, mounted on the wall behind the door. She had walked right by it on her way in without knowing it was there!

We often have gifts we don't notice—spiritual gifts that are right under our noses. Jesus has given them to us as Christians, yet we may not know we have them until someone points them out. As Paul wrote,

> But to each one of us grace was given according to the measure of Christ's gift...And He gave some as apostles, and some as prophets, and some as evangelists, and some as pastors and teachers, for the equipping of the saints for the work of service, to the building up of the body of Christ; until we all attain to the unity of the faith, and of the knowledge of the Son of God,

to a mature man, to the measure of the stature which belongs to the fullness of Christ (Eph 4:7, 11–13).

This scripture reveals at least four things to keep in mind in any discussion of spiritual gifts. First, these gifts come from Christ. He is the One who "ascended on high" (v. 8). Thus, any special spiritual abilities you have were given to you by him.

Second, Christ granted these gifts to celebrate his victory over sin, as Paul points out in the same chapter. Try to picture this in your mind. It is as if Jesus Christ were a conquering general in battle. When he ascended into heaven, he led behind him the captives of death and hell and sin, which he conquered when he rose from the dead, because they no longer have power over him or his followers. Jesus gave spiritual gifts to us as part of his victory celebration. In New Testament times, as a conquering general rode through the streets in his victory parade, he tossed trophies of battle to his supporters who stood along the way—silver, gold, precious fabrics, and other objects he had captured. People clamored for these like children scrambling for candy. It was the custom of the day. And this is exactly what Jesus did when he ascended into heaven: He tossed out the trophies of battle to you and me. What were those trophies? Spiritual gifts.

The third thing to remember about spiritual gifts is that a Christian receives special ability to do whatever God calls him to do. Notice again that Ephesians 4:12 says our spiritual gifts are "for the equipping of the saints for the work of service." You don't need to worry about being able to answer God's calling, because he will equip you to do the task.

My brother used to be a company clerk for the Quartermaster Corps at Fort Benning, Georgia. As raw recruits came into the induction station, it was Dan's job to muster out their gear. Every new soldier was equipped for service with a uniform, pack, shovel, pair of shoes, and so on. Imagine that Jesus Christ is your spiritual Quartermaster. When you report for duty in his Kingdom, he equips you for duty. That is what the Bible says here.

The fourth point Paul makes is that Jesus grants spiritual gifts for "building up the Body of Christ." He gives you special abilities not for your benefit, but to benefit other Christians. They are service abilities, not self-service abilities.

The same could be said of any gift. When you plunge into the crowd at a shopping mall to find a Christmas gift for someone, your first thought is, "What would she really like?" But your second thought is, "What would benefit the people around her?" If you think I am exaggerating, consider some gifts that might have been under your Christmas tree last year. That bottle of perfume for your aunt, for example, had a delightful fragrance. You knew she would enjoy wearing it because she likes the scent, but don't the people around her enjoy it, too? Most gifts benefit the people who receive them and other people as well. So it is with spiritual gifts.

I underscore this point because I think some of us spend too much time attending seminars and reading books that help us develop our spiritual gifts without employing them for the good of the Body. As a result, new Christians don't care to discover their gifts because it seems a self-centered hobby. Christ gives spiritual gifts

# Discover Your Gifts

to equip the saints and build up the Body. He makes sure that no Christian has all the service gifts. He distributes them throughout the fellowship, so we have to depend on each other. What an ingenious plan!

## *Gifts vs. Talents*

Some people have an innate ability to talk in a constructive way. They have the talent known as loquacity. They can begin a conversation and keep it going; they know interesting things to talk about; and they can draw creative ideas of other persons.

Some people have the innate ability of listening, too, which is just as important. (If God had not given as many people the ability to listen as he did the ability to talk, it would be a frustrating world, wouldn't it?) But inborn abilities are not what Paul is talking about in his letter to the Ephesians. The text describes gifts Christ gave us when he triumphed over sin; and that triumph applies to us only after we are converted. Christ's victory means nothing for you until you give your heart to him. At that moment, you receive the gifts he made available. You receive his special equipment "for works of service" (Eph 4:12).

It is usually harder to discern spiritual gifts than natural abilities such as loquacity. We tend to praise a Christian's talents since they are obvious, but we may stumble over one another's spiritual gifts quite by accident. We do not know that the quiet, smartly dressed young woman who sits in the back pew has a gift for administration until we ask her to organize a telephone campaign. We don't know that the balding, fiftyish bachelor has a gift for teaching until we ask him to substitute for the junior high Sunday school teacher one morning. Talents are obvious, but spiritual gifts are hidden. I believe many churches have burned out more than a few willing workers because they have not tried to discover and employ more of their congregations' spiritual gifts.

### *The Goal of God's Church*

Ephesians 4:13 says we should use our spiritual gifts in serving one another so that we may attain "the measure of the stature which belongs to the fullness of Christ." This is the goal of the church. Individually and as a body, we are called to become like Christ himself. Many years ago, C.W. Naylor wrote a song entitled "More Like Christ." Here is the first stanza:

> More like Christ my heart is praying,
> More like Christ from day to day,
> All his graces rich displaying
> While I tread this pilgrim way.

Every Christian should aim to become more like Christ, who is the measure of spiritual maturity. It is important for each of us to discover and develop our God-given gifts that help all of us become more like Christ. The apostle Paul told his young friend Timothy to "fan into flame the gift of God, which is in you." (2 Tim 1:6). You have been specially gifted to help other Christians grow, so when you have identified that gift, do everything you can to enhance it. Fan the spark of your spiritual gift into a blazing flame for Christ.

Do you suppose some Christians have no gift? Then read Ephesians 4:7: "To each one of us grace has been given as Christ apportioned it." Every Christian has a spiritual gift. Christ himself chose the gift that would be best for you,

# Discover Your Gifts

the one you could use to glorify him most fully.

The Lord has no unequipped servants. To put it another way, he has no "generic" Christians. Supermarkets now carry a wide array of generic products: canned foods, boxed cereals, facial tissues, paper towels and other items with no brand names. Generics often come in rather unimaginative packaging to emphasize the fact that they are cheaper; they have no color, no flair, no special features highlighted. They are presented as being the basic, generic "stuff."

But each Christian is unique. Jesus Christ has given you service gifts that set you apart from every other Christian. Perhaps you have failed to notice your gifts, and perhaps they have never been employed, but the Word of God guarantees that you have them!

## *Let's Take Inventory*

Arlo F. Newell has given us an instructive study of spiritual gifts in his book *Receive the Holy Spirit*[2]. He notes three general classes of New Testament spiritual gifts:

- Speaking gifts (e.g., prophesying and teaching)
- Serving gifts (e.g., administration and helping)
- Signifying gifts (e.g., tongues and miracles)[3]

These classifications are easy to remember and they prompt us to think about our talents as well. A Christian with a talent for counseling can listen intently while someone describes a personal problem and then offer good advice; his speaking gift helps that person grow. Another Christian with a talent for playing musical instruments can do much to enhance a worship service; her serving gift helps us grow. The Bible does not list counseling or playing instruments among the spiritual gifts, but they certainly enhance other Christians' maturity in Christ.

Here's a pen-and-paper exercise to help you take inventory of your spiritual gifts, using Dr. Newell's categories:

| *Formal Church Life* | *Informal Church Life* |
|---|---|
|  |  |

Under the heading "Formal Church Life," give a brief description of every official church duty you have performed. (Include teaching a class, making announcements in a worship service, counseling someone in a prayer room, serving refreshments, washing dishes after potluck dinners—everything!) Put an asterisk (*) beside each one that you seemed to have a special knack for doing.

Under the section "Informal Church Life," describe everything you have done to serve your Christian brothers and sisters outside the church's normal weekly

**Discover Your Gifts**

routine, those spur-of-the-moment duties you have performed for other Christians on the impulse of love. Examples might be staying at the bedside of a sick friend, preparing a meal for a bereaved family, writing cards of encouragement, counseling someone over the phone, and so on. Again, put an asterisk beside each function that you seemed to do especially well.

Now list every duty you marked with an asterisk under one of the three spiritual gift types.

| *Speaking Gifts* | *Serving Gifts* | *Signifying Gifts* |
|---|---|---|
|  |  |  |

Here is an example of how your list might look:

| *Speaking Gifts* | *Serving Gifts* | *Signifying Gifts* |
|---|---|---|
| *Teaching S.S. Class | *Washing Dishes | *Praying for Healing |
| *Visiting Absentees | *Mending Curtains | |

Are more of your items clustered under one heading? This suggests your spiritual gifts lie in that area. The sample above belongs to a person with strong serving gifts; if he tries to engage in other kinds of personal service, he might uncover even more gifts.

The best way to discover your spiritual gifts is to exercise them by trying them out in your local congregation. I hope you worship with a group of Christians who will risk letting you try something you have never tried before. You might fail. On the other hand, you might prove to have an extraordinary gift you didn't even know about!

Early in this book, I said that developing your goals and plans might be likened to developing a photograph. Spiritual gifts are the darkroom equipment of your life; they bring out the character traits God gave you. Renowned nature photographer Ansel Adams was able to render a particular scene in a variety of ways by using the same negative but different chemicals, filters, and papers in the darkroom. Adams himself said, "The negative is the score. The print is the performance." So it is with spiritual gifts: Your life goal is your score, but you can render it any number of ways, depending on how you employ your spiritual gifts.

### *Duty and Delight*

Every gift brings responsibilities. The Christian who discovers his gifts feels uncomfortable till he begins using them as the Lord intended. He is like the Old Testament prophet who said that prophecy was "like a burning fire shut up in my bones" (Jer 20:9).

Every gift has its privileges, too. News reporters in Washington, D.C., have long complained about the special privileges that come with high office: private limousine service, heated pools, plush lounges, trips abroad. But some executive privileges are essential. Who would quarrel with the President's need for a bodyguard or the Senators' need for couriers?

Consider the executive privileges that Christians have. A Christian with the gift of praying for the sick has the privilege of seeing them healed. A Christian with the gift of counseling has the thrill of seeing people find God's will for their lives. A Christian with the gift of administration has the satisfaction of resolving difficult problems within the church. When you feel weighed down by your duties in the Body of Christ, remember your gifts! And relish their privileges—executive privileges!

---

1. M. Blaine Smith, *Knowing God's Will* (Downers Grove, Ill.: InterVarsity Press, 1979), 98.

2. Arlo F. Newell, *Receive the Holy Spirit* (Anderson, Ind.: Warner Press, 1978), 90.

3. The signifying gifts are commonly called "charismatic" gifts. I dislike that phrase because it singles out a few spiritual gifts as if they were of a different quality than the rest. The word *charismatic* means "pertaining to gifts." All spiritual gifts, therefore, might be called charismatic because all are given by God.

*Some of us may be fearing the wrong thing. What we fear most is the pain that is necessary for our own growth.*
—*William E. Hulme*[1]

## 10. When You Need to Change Your Plans

A widow I knew began making some bold changes in her life plans. Her children had married or gone away to college, and she had no further obligations, so she decided to sell her house to begin helping other people wherever she might be needed. She spent several months caring for an invalid friend in Fort Wayne. She helped her oldest son start a new congregation in Virginia. She served as a cook at a Christian retreat center in Tennessee. Then she worked at a Christian nursery school in Louisville.

The next time we met at a Christmas Eve service, I said, "You're like the wise men following the star. They didn't know their destination. They just knew they were going in the right direction."

Perhaps that describes your life, too. You may feel God leading you to change your life plans. Your circumstances may have changed so abruptly that you feel a little puzzled about how things will turn out, but you are sure you are going in the right direction.

The apostle Paul had this experience. He knew God wanted him to be a bold spokesman for Jesus Christ and a shepherd of new Christian congregations springing up throughout the Roman world, but God changed his specific plans many times. Indeed, Paul's life ended much sooner than he expected and in a way he did not expect, yet he knew these changes were part of God's purpose for his life. He knew his

# When You Need to Change Your Plans

life was going in the right direction, even when the executioner's axe fell.

### *A Change of Itinerary*

The first chapter of 2 Corinthians describes one of these unexpected changes in Paul's plans. Paul was making his third missionary journey, visiting the churches scattered around the Mediterranean. He planned to go to Corinth, a troubled church, to see if they had made any progress toward resolving the problems he observed in his first visit with them. Then he planned to proceed to Macedonia, make a circuit of the churches in that region, and finally return to Corinth to receive an offering for the famine-stricken churches in Judea.

But while Paul was visiting the churches in Asia Minor, he was stricken with a grave health problem. He writes of "the troubles we experienced in the province of Asia" (2 Cor 1:8), saying that "we were under great pressure, far beyond our ability to endure, so that we despaired of life itself."

Perhaps Paul had a physical or emotional collapse, exhausted by the nerve-wracking schedule. Perhaps he had a flare-up of his "thorn in the flesh," an unidentified malady he mentions later in 2 Corinthians 12:7–10. Perhaps he had a heart attack or stroke. Whatever his affliction, Paul says only that it required a long period of recovery.

This health trouble gave Paul time to think. He decided not to visit Corinth after all and sent his young associate Titus instead. He told his Corinthian friends that he had decided, on second thought, not to check up on them because they might grow more mature if he spared them a "bawling out."

Circumstances had forced a change in Paul's plan and reflection showed him what the change should be. God confirmed that the change would glorify him. Paul explains in his letter to the Corinthians two different ways he sensed the Lord's confirmation of his new plan. First, God gave him confidence.

> Our conscience testifies that we have conducted ourselves in the world, and especially in our relations with you, with integrity and godly sincerity. We have done so, relying not on worldly wisdom but on God's grace (2 Cor 1:12).

Paul had a clear conscience about changing his plans; He knew he had made his decision with sincere, God-fearing intent. The pastor of a congregation we attended in Nashville, Tennessee, often closed a worship service by asking, "Are all hearts clear?" He knew God was convicting the hearts of some people who had heard the gospel preached that day, yet they had refused to make a clear decision. So Pastor Newton offered that final challenge. God will give you a clear conscience when you are doing his will. He will assure you that, even though you have had to change your course of action, you are doing the right thing.

The second way God confirmed Paul's decision was by showing him positive results. Paul congratulated the Corinthians, "for it is by faith you stand firm" (v. 24). He had yearned to see the Corinthians grow up, emotionally and spiritually, and by canceling his plans to visit them he had forced them to take responsibility for their actions. Granted, they were still immature in many respects, but they were staying true to Jesus Christ. This result alone told Paul he had made the right decision.

Notice that Paul does not say God used a dream, vision, or prophetic revelation to specify what to do, although in other epistles he talks freely about receiving guidance through those channels. Instead, Paul says he made the decision "in holiness and godly sincerity." While following the intentions of a sincere, godly heart, Paul considered the facts, reviewed what he hoped to accomplish for the Lord, and concluded that the best way to achieve his purpose was to cancel his trip to Corinth.

Notice, too, that Paul made his decision before he had God's guarantee that it was the best plan. Both confirmations—his clear conscience and the good results—came after Paul's decision to bypass Corinth. We usually have to make our decisions with the facts in hand and a heart burning to do what is right. Although God will confirm our decision afterward, at the moment of decision we have to trust our own best judgment. M. Blaine Smith writes:

> In the overwhelming majority of decisions noted in the New Testament God's will was discerned through a reasoned decision. Human reason was the channel through which God's will was normally known; discerning his will boiled down to a matter of making a sound, logical choice.[2]

We might debate whether it was actually God who changed Paul's plans. What if Paul revised his plans simply because of the circumstances, as a matter of expediency? Circumstances don't always reveal the will of God, do they? Indeed they don't, but circumstances may force us to reconsider our plans. If Paul had not fallen ill, he might have camped in Corinth for months, trying to untangle the problems of that church. Paul's illness also forced him to reconsider his plans; it challenged him to ask God if there be a better way to help the Corinthians.

We can debate whether God caused Paul his "great adversity," but one thing is clear: God prevailed upon Paul in the adversity to find a better plan of action. He guided Paul's heart. Paul chose a better plan because adversity prompted further thinking, and a holy heart guided his thinking.

### Modern Examples of Revised Plans

It is painful to change your plans, especially if you are emotionally invested in the original plan or you have talked it up with your friends. It is hard to change career plans, marital plans, or any other plan that you earnestly expect to fulfill. But God calls his servants to change their plans at times, no matter how ingenious and perfect those plans had seemed.

Circumstances may force such a change, as in the case of Joyce Landorf. She was forced to suspend a successful ministry of singing and lecturing because of a painful jaw ailment, only to discover a new and broader ministry of writing.

In other cases, we may opt for a change even though circumstances don't demand it. I remember having lunch with a good friend who was making an abrupt change in his career. He had been a pastor, then an editor at a Christian publishing house. At a retreat where he assessed his personal goals, he realized that he secretly

# When You Need to Change Your Plans

yearned to be a pastor again. An attractive college church asked him to consider becoming their pastor. He visited the church, saw how much he enjoyed using his pastoral gifts, and decided in a few days to accept their call.

"I'm surprised it happened so fast," he told me over tossed salad. "I knew I might go back to pastoral work someday, but I had told myself I would stick with the editorial job for at least two more years."

"Why?"

"I felt I owed that much to my publishing firm."

"So what convinced you to change your plans?"

"The Lord did," he smiled. "I would have betrayed the gifts he gave me if I stayed in publishing out of a sheer sense of duty. I'll have some regrets about leaving. There may even be days I'll wonder if I made the right decision. But I've decided to make the best of what the Lord has given me."

You might say my friend made an elective change of plans, since nothing forced him to do it. His superiors at the publishing house were pleased with his work; his wife and family were supportive; barring any unforeseen obstacles, he could have stayed there indefinitely. But he yielded to his God-given dream of returning to the pastorate.

You may be facing a change of plans right now. Whether it is an elective change or one forced by your circumstances, remember this: *You can still achieve your goals and become the person God expects you to be, even though the details of your future may not be what you had pictured.*

## Two Extremes to Avoid

Some people are too prone to change. They like to rearrange their careers, marriages, or friendships almost as often as they rearrange the furniture in their living rooms. The Bible says to avoid such people; they make life a shambles for themselves and for you (Prov 24:21). On the other end of the spectrum are people who refuse to change their life plans. They are miserable as they are, but afraid that a different way of life would be even more miserable. They say, "At least I know how to deal with the mess I'm in." So they grit their teeth and hang on.

A healthy, mature Christian lives between those two extremes. He does not change his lifestyle flippantly every few months, but he does not dig in his heels and refuse to change, either. A healthy Christian accepts change as a natural part of life. He is flexible enough to adapt to adversity and ambitious enough to take opportunity. Either way, he pursues the personal goals that he believes will best honor the Lord.

### *God's Will, God's Word, and Your Plans*

When you need to change your life plans, you come to grips with a question that has occupied theologians for centuries: How can I know God's will for my life? Instead of trying to provide a pat answer, I invite you once again to use your imagination. How do you visualize God revealing His will to you?

Do you see him writing you a letter, setting down explicit directions in A-B-C fashion? "God has already given me a set of directions like that," you might say. "It's called the Bible." But that oversimplifies things a bit. God has provided his written Word to all people of the world, so you cannot expect to open the Bible and find a list of personal assignments for a certain day.

Of course, some Christians like to think they can use the Bible in that way. They suppose the Bible has mystical

## When You Need to Change Your Plans

power to direct their lives. If they want guidance for a specific decision, they browse through the Bible, or open it at random until they find a text that seems to give them the answer. That's treating the Bible as if it were a kind of divine Ouija board. It is not. The Bible does indeed contain God's general commands for all mankind and his specific commands for individual Christians. It says, for example, that marriage is an honorable option for any person (Heb 13:4), while it warns that a Christian should not marry an unsaved person (2 Cor 6:14). But the Bible does not say whether you should marry, neither does it specify which mate you should choose. In these matters, you must seek God's will directly from him.

If God's will does not come to us as a neat set of written directions, how does it come? Paul E. Little suggests it's like this:

> The will of God is...like a scroll that unrolls every day. In other words, God has a will for you and me today and tomorrow and the next day and the day after that...It may well be that a decision we make this week or next week will commit us for three months, or two years, or five or ten years, or for a lifetime. But the fact still remains that the will of God is something to be discerned and to be lived out each day of our lives. It is not something to be grasped as a package once for all.[3]

I like this scroll analogy. When a Jewish rabbi searches for a verse on one of the huge synagogue scrolls, he spools the parchment patiently from one spindle to the other until he finds the place. He can see only a small portion of the text at one time, although he knows the rest is there, wound on the rolls.

That is usually how we perceive God's plan for our lives, too. We see only the immediate plan—what he leads us to do today—even though we know there is more not yet revealed.

If we imagine God's will as a scroll, unrolling a bit more every day, we can expect some surprises now and then. Our lives will be full of unexpected changes. Our goals may seem always beyond our grasp, challenging us to grow. But we continue on because we have decided that our future is worth the pain and frustration of change today.

The French theologian Teilhard de Chardin said, "Since I started following Jesus, he has led me places I never expected to go." Every Christian could say that. Life is full of surprises when you are traveling with Jesus!

---

1. William E. Hulme, *Dealing with Double-Mindedness* (New York: Harper & Row, 1982), 24.

2. M. Blaine Smith, *Knowing God's Will* (Downers Grove, Ill.: InterVarsity Press, 1979), 61.

3. Paul E. Little, *Affirming the Will of God* (Downers Grove, Ill.: InterVarsity Press, 1971), 7–8.

*Start to live the kind of life God can bless, where you are. Don't wait until next month or next year for the opportunity that may make you great.* —Robert A. Cook[1]

# 11. Face Forward—It's Time to Start!

Economic and cultural changes in our world have forced many Christians to reexamine their goals and plans. Factories have shut down, throwing thousands of people out of work, and in many cases, those jobs have simply disappeared. I remember when International Harvester (now known as Navistar) began laying off a work force of more than ten thousand people in Fort Wayne, Indiana. Every kind of worker was affected—brawny men who worked on the assembly line and brilliant engineers who labored in the front office. But they all said, "What's to worry? Business will pick up in a few months. They'll call us back to work." The heavy truck business did not pick up, however, and three years later officials announced the Fort Wayne plant would be closed and sold. Thousands of laid-off Fort Wayne workers sat at home, stunned by the news. Their industry had changed and now they, too, had to change. (More than a decade would pass before General Motors opened a truck assembly plant in the city. It called for workers who knew how to operate a robotic assembly line, vastly different from the old Harvester factory. Few of the laid-off workers were able to qualify for jobs there.)

Family patterns have also undergone tremendous change. No longer can we take for granted the traditional image of the family we saw in Norman Rockwell's cover drawings for the *Saturday Evening Post*—a father, mother, two grandparents, and rosy-cheeked children sitting down to a festive table laden with food. That seldom happens anymore. There may be only one parent at the head of the table; the menu is probably more meager; and the grandparents may live far across the country. Our families have changed, and now we must change.

Medical science has changed our way of life, too. New technology and drugs allow us to fight off diseases and recover from accidents that would have claimed our lives not long ago. We may have a retirement that lasts twenty-five years or more. Many of us will spend part of our lives in a nursing home or other extended-care facility. Mentally or physically handicapped relatives may be able to live at home now, since we have the equipment and medication to care for them there. In each case, these medical advances bring dramatic changes in our lifestyle. Our physical lives have changed, and now we must change.

We are experiencing more radical changes than any generation has ever known. At the same time, we have more options than any generation has known. Necessity and opportunity are like the two wedges of a vise, squeezing our lives out of their old shape. But what will be the new shape of our lives? How can we set goals that will be reasonable, achievable, and pleasing to the Lord? These are the questions we have been attempting to answer.

### *No Future in the Past*

One thing is certain: We cannot construct our future by trying to patch up the past. If we try, we find ourselves in the predicament of the American novelist Thomas Wolfe, who grew up in the quaint mountain town of Asheville, North Carolina. After making a successful career in the North, he decided to visit Asheville again. It had changed. No longer a sleepy little village in the foothills of the Appalachians, it had become a bustling trade center and neon-lit tourist attraction. The novelist concluded sadly that the town he now wanted to see existed only in his memory; the real Asheville was very different from the one he remembered.

Thomas Wolfe was different, too. Strangers hailed him on the street and clamored for his autograph. Ambitious young writers pursued him with their manuscripts. He felt as though he were on public exhibit. No longer could he enjoy the quiet solitude he had known as a youth sitting on a park bench in Asheville. So Wolfe returned to New York and wrote the book *You Can't Go Home Again*, a kind of personal confession. He learned he could not return to the past, no matter how desperately he tried.

None of us can. We may want to recapture the past because it is familiar and predictable and safe. But regardless of how hard we try, we cannot live in the past. The surroundings are different and we are different. We may try to pick up life where we left off twenty years before, but it's no use. We cannot resurrect the past.

The Pharisees once asked why Jesus' disciples did not act like those of John the Baptist. Jesus replied,

> "No one sews a patch of unshrunk cloth on an old garment. Otherwise, the new piece will pull away from the old, making the tear worse. And no one pours new wine into old

wineskins. Otherwise, the wine will burst the skins, and both the wine and the wineskins will be ruined. No, they pour new wine into new wineskins" (Mark 2:21-22).

Jesus called his disciples to a completely new way of life—a freer, more joyful one. The traditionalists could not understand this. They thought that if certain disciplines had been good enough for John's disciples, they should be good enough for anyone, but Jesus freed his followers from conformity. He encouraged them to adopt a lifestyle that allowed them to serve him most faithfully, even if other holy men did not live that way!

Please understand. I am not telling you to adopt some exotic lifestyle to prove you are a Christian. I am not saying you should offend traditionalists to demonstrate that you are divinely chosen. That is not what Jesus meant. His point was this: Honoring the past and honoring other people are not a Christian's top priority. Honoring the Lord is.

I believe we honor the Lord by answering his "upward call" into the future. The apostle Paul lived this way. Near the end of his life, he wrote to his Christian friends at Philippi, encouraging them to stay true to the Lord. "I consider everything a loss because of the surpassing worth of knowing Christ Jesus my Lord," he wrote in Philippians 3:8. Even though he had experienced many wonderful spiritual victories in the past, he dared not dwell on the "good old days."

> Forgetting what is behind and straining toward what is ahead, I press on toward the goal to win the prize for which God has

called me heavenward in Christ Jesus. (Phil 3:13-14).

God was calling him upward, onward, and forward, so Paul did not intend to rest on his laurels. No, he was going forward with Christ! Paul lived vibrantly and radiantly in that spirit until the day of his death. So long as he followed the upward call of Christ, he had challenging new goals and plans for each day.

I believe God wants every Christian to live this way. He expects us to reflect his character more perfectly every day of our lives. I believe he intends for us to be goal-oriented, future-tending people who strive to become more like Him.

### "That Sounds Good, But..."

You may feel intimidated by the whole idea of goal-setting, especially if it challenges you to make radical changes in the way you live. I understand how you feel. I have often felt the same way. But when I read how other people made dramatic life changes for the Lord, I take courage to dream godly dreams and set godly goals.

The saints of Bible times were also uneasy about setting godly goals. In fact, when God gave them stirring dreams for the future, they often made excuses not to dream. Excuses like:

*"I'm too old."* The priest Zacharias prayed for a son so long that he assumed his prayer could not be answered. Then one day an angel appeared to him at the altar and predicted his wife would bear a son. "How can I be sure of this?" Zacharias asked in wonder. "I am an old man and my wife is well along in years" (Luke 1:18). Yet the old priest's wife bore a son, John the Baptist.

Zacharias became a father at an age long after most men would despair of having children.

***"I don't have what it takes."*** When God called Moses to confront the pharaoh of Egypt, he replied, "I am slow of speech and tongue" (Ex 4:10). He did not feel he could speak persuasively enough to the mighty builder of the pyramids. But God said, "Who gave human beings their mouths?...Is it not I, the Lord? Now go; I will help you speak and will teach you what to say" (vv. 11-12). Moses learned he did not have to be an eloquent speaker, just a faithful one. Then God gave him what to say.

***"I'm too committed to this way of life."*** Simon Peter knew Jesus was calling him to be a disciple and for a long time he was able to evade Jesus' call. But when he saw Jesus' miracles, he had to say something. "Go away from me, Lord," he cried, "I am a sinful man!" (Lk 5:8). He would rather keep on tending his nets more easily than embark on a totally new way of life. But the Lord said, "Don't be afraid; from now on you will fish for people" (v. 10).

Do these excuses sound familiar? They do to me, because I have used them myself! But Jesus Christ calls us forward. He calls us to let go of what is behind; that is forgiven. He calls us to reach out toward the dream; that is foreseen. He calls us to shape our character after his; that is foremost in His will for our lives.

A goal-oriented life may be painful. It may be checkered with failure and disappointment. But Christ promises great reward when we walk with him, face forward to eternity.

> Then Jesus said to his disciples: "Therefore I tell you, do not worry about your life, what

you will eat; or about your body, what you will wear. For life is more than food, and the body more than clothes…

"And do not set your heart on what you will eat or drink; do not worry about it. For the pagan world runs after all such things, and your Father knows that you need them. But seek his kingdom, and these things will be given to you as well.

"Do not be afraid, little flock, for your Father has been pleased to give you the kingdom" (Luke 12:22-23, 29-32).

At the beginning of this book, you may have viewed goal-setting in terms of material goals—what type of job you would like to have, what kind of home you would like to own, what style of clothes you would like to wear. But these things are not the heart of your future; they are merely the background details. The heart of the matter is this: *What sort of person will you become?*

To live as a servant of the King, reflecting the character of the King—that is the essence of Christian living. The Father has chosen gladly to give you that kind of living. You can begin fulfilling that goal today.

---

1. Robert A. Cook, *Now That I Believe* (Chicago: Moody Press, 1949), 107.

www.ingramcontent.com/pod-product-compliance
Lightning Source LLC
Chambersburg PA
CBHW071005080526
44587CB00015B/2355